To followers of Jesus working in politics,
including many in our church,
who endeavor daily to honor God
in the halls of government.

CONTENTS

Introduction

I woke up one Sunday morning for what I thought would be a normal day of worship with my church family in metropolitan Washington, D.C. I had just finished my sermon and stepped to the side of the stage to spend a couple of moments in quiet reflection as we prepared to take the Lord's Supper. The silence was broken, though, by a voice calling my name backstage with a sense of urgency. I stepped back into a dark area behind a curtain where two of our pastors met me with a man I didn't recognize.

"This is a representative from the White House," one of our pastors told me, turning to the man I didn't know. "The president is on his way to our service. He will be here in about five minutes, and they would like for us to pray for him."

As my eyes slowly adjusted to the dark, thoughts came flooding to my mind. We have congregants from over 100 different countries with a variety of political perspectives and positions, and we do everything possible to unify around Jesus alone in the church. Amidst a divisive political climate, I knew bringing the president on stage would lead to a myriad of different reactions both inside and outside our church family.

The White House representative looked at me, waiting for a response, and the thought that rose to the top of my mind was a passage from 1 Timothy 2. There, God commands us to pray

> *for kings and all who are in high positions, that we may lead*
> *a peaceful and quiet life, godly and dignified in every way.*
> *This is good, and it is pleasing in the sight of God our Savior, who*
> *desires all people to be saved and to come to the knowledge of the*
> *truth.* 1 TIMOTHY 2:2–4

I looked at the White House representative and agreed to bring the president on stage for prayer.

The representative turned and continued coordinating security protocols that were already in motion, and I returned to the stage. I led the Lord's Supper as I normally do, and we began singing one more song while I walked off to the side to wait for the president. It was my first moment to pause and process what was happening, and my head was spinning. It didn't have time to stop, though, because in a matter of seconds, the president appeared backstage.

I won't go into the details of our conversation in the brief moments before the prayer, but I will say that the president was both kind and cordial. As the final song of our service drew to a close, I walked out to address our congregation, as they were oblivious to what was happening. I began by reminding them of something I had just said at the end of my sermon—that our unity in the church revolves not around our ethnicity or politics but around Jesus and his Word. Then I read 1 Timothy 2:1–6, and I told those gathered that we had a unique opportunity to put God's Word into practice by praying over President Trump.

I invited the president to join me on the platform, and he walked out. The press corps that travels with him had assembled in front of the stage, and the sound of snapping cameras filled the shocked room. The president folded his hands in front of him, I placed my hand on his shoulder, and I began to pray.

I praised Jesus as the universal Lord and King over all, and I pleaded for his mercy in our country. I prayed specifically for the president and his family. I prayed that they would know God's love through the gospel and that he would govern with wisdom and justice for the good of all people. I prayed for other leaders— for congress, court officials, and others who serve at the national, state, and local levels. I concluded by asking that God might grant our president grace to lead our country well.

When I finished, the president thanked me and walked off the stage without comment. As he left the building, I wrapped up the service by honoring two missionary heroes who were among us that day. Then we sent one another out like we do every Sunday, by reciting the Great Commission together.

As soon as the service was over, I rushed off to a piano recital for my kids. As I settled into a seat and began listening to them play, I knew what had happened would be received and perceived differently by a variety of different people. It didn't take long to confirm my hunch. As the recital wore on, my phone began blowing up. Text message after text message. A few phone calls.

Had I made the right decision?

That night, a group of our church leaders and their families gathered with my family for a previously scheduled dinner. As we ate, leaders shared about how different members of our church had experienced the day's events. Some were excited; others were disappointed. (If you can't imagine why someone would be either excited or disappointed about praying for the president on stage, then hang with me until Question 6, where I hope you'll be helped to understand both perspectives.) There was turmoil among the people, and it broke my heart. As a pastor who cares for every member of our church, I knew I needed to communicate what had happened and why I chose to invite President Trump to the stage for public prayer.

After the guests left, I spent the remainder of the night and well into Monday morning working on a letter to our church family. I emphasized how I only want to lead our church in a way that transcends political views and celebrates the unity we have in Christ amidst all of our differences. I put the final period on the letter, and we posted it online late Monday morning.

Little did I know that as a result of that prayer on Sunday, and the letter I posted on Monday, I would find myself at the center of a social media firestorm. Opinions were being expressed from all perspectives. Words were being twisted in all sorts of ways. I began getting countless requests from national news and television outlets. (I turned them all down.) Some said I approved of everything the president does (in case you're wondering, I don't). Others claimed I had apologized for praying for the president (in case you're wondering, I didn't). Turns out, on Sunday I made a lot of people glad while those on the other side of the aisle were mad. On Monday, however, I turned the tables—everyone who had been glad was suddenly mad. In less than 24 hours, I managed to be labeled *both* a far right-wing conservative *and* a far left-wing liberal.

That's not easy to do!

As I watched everything unfold, I couldn't help but draw one conclusion about the church amidst the political climate in our country: *we are sick.* We are so quick to accuse, belittle, cancel, distrust, disparage, deride, and divide from one another. And it's not just people outside the church; it's people inside the church, too. And it's not just this or that side; it's all of us, including me. We are swimming in toxic political waters that are poisoning the unity Jesus desires for his church, and we are polluting the glory Jesus deserves through us in the world.

That's why, just over a year after the president's visit to our church, I am compelled to write this short book as we approach a presidential election in our country. I don't want to see the church further divided or the name of Christ further defamed. Instead, I long to see a united church that exalts the name of Christ in this toxic political climate.

To this end, my aim in this book is not to endorse or denounce (or even hint toward supporting or opposing) any presidential candidate or political party. Yes, even as I write that, I can see eyes rolling. "I've heard this before," you sigh. "The pastor who says he's not going to tell me how to vote, but then sends me away with a Christian voter's guide that makes it clear that if I really love God, I'll vote in a particular way or down a particular party line."

I get the cynicism. Actually, I share it.

Moreover, I fully realize that some readers wish I would speak for or against a particular candidate or party, and they will (at least initially) be upset that I don't. I think about members and leaders in our church, as well as close friends of mine beyond our church, some of whom would say I should publicly criticize a particular candidate; others would say I should clearly condemn a particular party. Interestingly, however, many of these genuine followers of Jesus have conflicting ideas about who or what should be criticized or condemned.

In a country where the church is often divided over political positions, my purpose in this book is not more partisanship. My hope is to fuel deeper affection for Christ while fostering healthier conversations among Christians as we participate in a presidential election. Put another way, my chief concern in this book is not who wins on election day. My chief concern is infinitely more important. I'm concerned with where you stand in Christ and where we stand as the church on election day and in the days thereafter.

As a pastor of men and women who live in one of the most politically divisive metropolitan areas in the world, I sincerely long for each of them to wake up on election day with authentic love for Jesus, a counter-cultural unity in the church, and a clean and clear conscience about how they can honor God with their vote. Beyond the people I pastor, I want every follower of Jesus in this country, regardless of political affiliation, to experience this reality. As you read this book, I want *you* to experience this reality.

With that aim in mind, this book includes seven questions I'm convinced every follower of Jesus should ask and answer before voting. These questions are rooted in God's Word, our final authority in the Christian life. Even if you already know how you're planning to vote, I encourage you to answer these questions humbly and honestly before you cast your ballot. If you have no clue how you're going to vote, I hope answering these questions will help you in your decision. Regardless, my prayer is that by asking and answering these questions, you and I will grow in our relationship with Jesus as we resolve to glorify him together in a country that desperately needs what no presidential candidate or political party could ever give.

1

DOES GOD CALL ME TO VOTE?

IMAGINE LEADING a prayer in a normal Sunday morning service at our church. Look out across the auditorium. On one side you see one of the most prominent leaders in our country surrounded by Secret Service agents. On the other side, you see a cabinet member. In the middle, a senator sits with his family. On your left and right are cable news hosts from different networks. Scattered throughout the room are other legislators, lobbyists, lawyers, diplomats (including some from different countries), consultants, and all kinds of aides.

Of course, not everyone in the Sunday service works in politics. But when you think about it, they're all involved in politics, aren't they? Aren't they all affected by decisions that politicians make? And don't we live in a land where every man and woman has a voice in who our politicians are and what our politicians do? When you think about it this way, politics is not just a consideration for me as a pastor in metro Washington, D.C.; it affects every Christian in every church across our country.

This compels us to ask the question, "To what extent should American Christians use their voice in politics? Specifically, should every Christian vote?" This is the foundational question as we begin this journey, particularly because we have different ideas about how to answer it. After all, many Christians don't vote. Meanwhile, other Christians claim that it's our duty to vote. But is that true? Where in the Bible do we see a command to vote? Search the Scriptures, and you won't find one anywhere.

But does that mean this question is closed? Maybe not. Perhaps there are other commands from God that might lead us to conclude that voting brings glory to God. So let's take a step back and see what God says.

Delegation from God

From the beginning of the Bible, we learn that all governance ultimately belongs to God. He is the Supreme Creator of all, Sovereign Ruler over all, and Righteous Judge of all. In this way, God's Word cuts completely against the grain of how democratically-minded Americans are wired to think.

This world is not a democracy. This world is a monarchy, and God is the King. Sure, we may use language about our rights, and we may even compose and ascribe to a "Bill of Rights," but the reality is simple: God has all the rights, and we are subject to him.

At the same time, in a stunning demonstration of God's grace, he has entrusted authority and dominion over his creation to men and women made in his image. The Bible tells us,

> *God created man in his own image, in the image of God he created him; male and female he created them. And God blessed them. And God said to them, "Be fruitful and multiply and fill the earth and subdue it, and have dominion over the fish of the sea and over the birds of the heavens and over every living thing that moves on earth."* GENESIS 1:27–28

God gave dominion—or entrusted authority—to humans who have a unique capacity to relate to him and to reflect his rule in the world. The psalmist meditates on this amazing privilege:

> *You have made him a little lower than the heavenly beings and crowned him with glory and honor. You have given him dominion over the works of your hands; you have put all things under his feet, all sheep and oxen, and also the beasts of the field, the birds of the heavens, and the fish of the sea, whatever passes along the paths of the seas.* PSALM 8:5–8

According to the Bible, God has put the world under our feet. He has given us the responsibility to oversee it in a way that aligns with his Word and accords with his character.

Our Need for Grace

Sadly, however, we have not carried out this responsibility in a way that aligns with God's Word and accords with his character. Just three chapters into the Bible, we see the pride of a man and a woman who defy the governing authority of God. The result of this sinful defiance is total disorder in the world—a shattered relationship with God, contentious relationships with one another, and a cursed relationship with creation.

Doesn't the story of Scripture make sense of our current world climate? If all governance belongs to God, and he delegates governance to people, and those people defy him, then no government in this world can be perfectly good, for every government is led by people who have rebelled against God. Such rebellion is the source of every problem in the world, including every problem in government. Put plainly, all those who govern (and all those who are governed) are sinners, so to have any hope of experiencing God's good design for government, we are in desperate need of God's grace.

Foundations for Governance

Thankfully, God is generous with his grace. As sin multiplies in the world through the opening pages of Scripture, God enables people—even people who don't necessarily follow him—to administer justice by promoting good, punishing evil, and protecting people from harm. In a fundamental restart of society after the flood, God establishes essential foundations for just governance in the world.[1] He says in Genesis 9,

> *For your lifeblood I will require a reckoning: from every beast I will require it and from man. From his fellow man I will require a reckoning for the life of man. "Whoever sheds the blood of man, by man shall his blood be shed, for God made man in his own image. And you, be fruitful and multiply, increase greatly on the earth and multiply in it."* GENESIS 9:5–7

According to these verses, God has created all people equally in his image, and he requires us to do justice so that every single person might flourish in the world.

As I read Genesis 9, I can almost hear God saying, "Okay, everyone, listen up. This is your responsibility together. Make sure that justice is carried out for everybody. This is a task I am entrusting to all of you." Do you see what's happening here? God is delegating the responsibility for protecting each other and for prosecuting crimes that bring harm to one another. And he's delegating it to us.

Importantly, and as no small aside, God does not give people the responsibility to prosecute all crimes that bring dishonor to him. God gives systems of governance to humankind in order to punish things like stealing or murder, but not things like selfish pride or false religion. Selfish pride and false religion are without question crimes against God, but God retains sole responsibility for judging those crimes. Put another way, God is not asking us to run his theocracy.

For the Good of People

Understanding these foundations, it is no surprise to turn to the New Testament and read the following words in Romans 13:1–7:

> *Let every person be subject to the governing authorities. For there is no authority except from God, and those that exist have been instituted by God. Therefore whoever resists the authorities resists what God has appointed, and those who resist will incur judgment. For rulers are not a terror to good conduct, but to bad. Would you have no fear of the one who is in authority? Then do what is good, and you will receive his approval, for he is God's servant for your good. But if you do wrong, be afraid, for he does not bear the sword in vain. For he is the servant of God, an avenger who carries out God's wrath on the wrongdoer. Therefore one must be in subjection, not only to avoid God's wrath but also for the sake of conscience. For because of this you also pay taxes, for the authorities are ministers of God, attending to this very thing. Pay to all what is owed to them:*

taxes to whom taxes are owed, revenue to whom revenue is owed, respect to whom respect is owed, honor to whom honor is owed.

Likewise, in 1 Peter 2:13–17, one of Jesus's closest followers writes,

Be subject for the Lord's sake to every human institution, whether it be to the emperor as supreme, or to governors as sent by him to punish those who do evil and to praise those who do good. For this is the will of God, that by doing good you should put to silence the ignorance of foolish people. Live as people who are free, not using your freedom as a cover-up for evil, but living as servants of God. Honor everyone. Love the brotherhood. Fear God. Honor the emperor.

Both passages expand upon what we have already seen in God's Word, which we could summarize in two foundational statements.

Foundational Statement Number One:

Government is a God-ordained institution for the purpose of promoting good and restraining evil. The purpose of government is to provide for the good of people and to punish bad conduct among people. By the design of God, government "bears the sword," meaning government has the authority to enforce laws and penalize law-breakers.

Foundational Statement Number Two:

Followers of Jesus should be submissive citizens of government with ultimate allegiance to God. We'll unpack the second part of that statement in the next question, but staying focused on the first part, Scripture is clear that we are to subject ourselves to the government as a God-ordained authority over us. As part of that subjection, we are to support our government by paying taxes, revenue, respect, and honor to our governing authorities.

In all of this, we realize that government, by God's design, possesses significant power and influence in the world. When such power and influence are used in accord with the justice of God, government is a gracious instrument in God's hand for the flourishing of all people made in his image.

Divine Requirements

Are there any other requirements God gives us in his Word regarding government? Well, God specifically commands his people to do justice for one another. We will explore more about what it means to do justice in Question 3, but I will simply define justice here as that which is right for all people as exemplified in the character of God and expressed in the Word of God.

With this biblical definition of justice in mind, hear God's words to his people in Jeremiah 22:3, "Do justice and righteousness," and in Micah 6:8, "He has told you, O man, what is good; and what does the Lord require of you but to do justice, and to love kindness, and to walk humbly with your God?" This is strong language from God. He requires, commands, and—in a very real sense—demands that his people do justice.

> "Do justice and righteousness."
> Jeremiah 22:3

God also commands his people to seek the welfare of the nation in which they live. This was not only the case when Israel inhabited the Promised Land, but it was also God's command to them when they were living in a foreign land as a result of the exile. Scattered among the nations, God told them, "Seek the welfare of the city where I have sent you into exile, and pray to the Lord on its behalf, for in its welfare you will find your welfare" (Jeremiah 29:7). God instructed his people to pray for the nation of their exile while working for the well-being of that nation.

When we come to the New Testament, God's requirements for his people, the church, are summed up in two commands: love God with all your heart, soul, mind, and strength, and love your neighbor as yourself (Mark 12:30–31). As followers of Jesus, God requires us to live with undivided love for him and unselfish love for all people around us. Surely such a way of life affects how we participate in city, state, and national governance.

Governed or Governing?

Before we draw all of this together to answer Question 1, "Does God call us to vote?" I should mention one other significant reality in light of what we've already seen from Scripture. For even asking this question about voting sets us apart from followers of Jesus in the Bible, as well as many followers of Jesus around the world today.

All throughout Scripture, God makes it clear that leaders in government are responsible to him and will be judged by him. From Moses's confrontation of Pharaoh in Egypt to Elijah's confrontation of King Ahab, from Nathan's confrontation of King David in Israel to John the Baptist's confrontation of King Herod in Judea, those who make governing decisions are accountable to God for their decisions. This is why Daniel confronts King Nebuchadnezzar in Babylon, saying, "Break off your sins by practicing righteousness, and your iniquities by showing mercy to the oppressed" (Daniel 4:27). In short, those who make decisions in government are responsible for the effects of those decisions on the people influenced by their governance.

These Scripture passages should give followers of Jesus who live in a representative democracy a sober sense of responsibility. By God's grace, he has given us a voice in who leads (or doesn't lead) us. He has given us a say in how laws are created and how justice is carried out in and through our country. The entire idea of a representative democracy—a government *of* the people, *by* the people, and *for* the people—means that we are not just the "governed" in Romans 13 and 1 Peter 2; in a very real sense, we are also the "governing." Our votes collectively shape our government.

Therefore, we are in a very different position today than the church in the first century. Followers of Jesus in the New Testament did not have a say in who led them and how they would be led. For that matter, neither do followers of Jesus in North Korea or many other nations in the world today. But we do. Consequently, as "governing" citizens we are accountable before God for the good of people affected by our government.

What's the Answer?

Now let's bring together all that we have seen from God's Word, and let's start by acknowledging again what we have *not* seen. There is no direct command from God in his Word to vote in an election. This is due in part to the reality that democratic elections did not exist in biblical times. Even still, we should carefully avoid saying that God requires something of us unless we have a clear biblical foundation for that statement.

So what does God require of us? According to our short survey of Scripture, we conclude that God requires people to do the following:

Reflect his just governance by working to promote good, punish evil, and protect all people from harm.
SEE GENESIS 1:27–28; 9:1–7; PSALM 8:5–8

Subject ourselves to and support government for the flourishing of all people. SEE ROMANS 13:1–7; 1 PETER 2:13–17

Do justice—that which is right for all people as exemplified in the character of God and expressed in the Word of God.
SEE JEREMIAH 22:3; MICAH 6:8

Pray and work for the welfare of the nation in which we live.
SEE JEREMIAH 29:7

Love God and love our neighbors as ourselves. SEE MATTHEW 22:37–40

Steward any responsibility we have in governance for the good of all people affected by our government.
SEE ROMANS 13:1–7; 1 PETER 2:13–17; DANIEL 4:27

Based upon the biblical commands above, and the unique grace that God has given us as followers of Jesus and "governing" citizens in a representative democracy, it seems we have a responsibility before God and one another to steward our vote for the sake of good, God-glorifying governance.

| Convictional Inaction or Action

Does that mean it is a sin not to vote? Not necessarily. First, again, I want to be extremely careful to only call sin that which God clearly calls sin. And second, it could be possible for followers of Jesus to make a prayerful, intentional decision to "steward their vote" by not voting. Let me explain.

I have heard followers of Jesus argue for convictional inaction, which is basically a conscious and deliberate refusal to support any political candidate, organization, or party. This is not the decision of the lazy who just don't get around to voting on election day. Nor is it the decision of those who throw up their hands in frustration and cast aside any sense of responsibility to use their vote or voice for the sake of just governance. Convictional inaction is based on the belief that if followers of Jesus would intentionally refrain from voting, then political candidates, organizations, and parties in the United States might make significant changes in order to woo their vote. In the long run, these Christians argue, this is a valid way of stewarding your vote for the sake of just governance through future elections as politicians are forced to listen to the concerns of the non-voting.

To be clear, I am not advocating for or against convictional inaction. My aim in even mentioning this option is to say that followers of Jesus will "steward their vote" in different ways. Still, let's not make a hasty decision about going the convictional inaction route

> "God calls us to use every means of grace he grants us to love him above all and love our neighbors as ourselves."

quite yet. After all, there may be some other factors to consider before deciding that the best way to do justice is by not voting.

In the end, what's most important, and what I am definitively advocating for based on God's Word, is the realization that how we use our vote is a matter of faithfulness before God. For our vote is a unique privilege and responsibility that God has entrusted to us by his grace, and God calls us to use every means of grace he grants us to love him above all and love our neighbors as ourselves.

QUESTION

2

WHO HAS MY HEART?

"NOW, I KNOW that every election people say, 'This is the most important election of our lifetime.' But this time, it actually is."

How many times have you heard that? I'm guessing your answer corresponds with the number of elections you've lived through. And I understand why. We really care about our country in the present and the future. We're besieged by the pressing needs around us as well as the pivotal issues ahead of us. We're panicked by the prospect of what will happen if this or that candidate gets elected, or this or that party gains power.

But what if there's another way to look at an election? What if there's a way to be free from worry about its outcome? What if there's a way to have true peace and total confidence no matter what takes place in our government? Is that possible?

I think about Fatima and Yaseen, friends of mine who live under a totalitarian Muslim regime that has outlawed conversion to Christianity. When Fatima placed her faith in Jesus, she knew she was risking her life and the loss of her family. Yaseen is a pastor of a secret church in a community not far from Fatima, and his house has been both raided and bombed. Yaseen and his family live under constant threat of governmental persecution.

Needless to say, Fatima and Yaseen have never considered putting their hope in their government. Similarly, their peace, joy, and confidence do not hinge on political leaders, platforms, or policies. Could we learn something from them?

Now some might say, "But Fatima and Yaseen would benefit greatly from the freedoms and protections we have as followers of Jesus in the United States." And I would agree. Still, others might say, "We're in danger of losing some of these freedoms and protections in the United States." That may also be true. But these comments miss the point. Even if we lose every freedom and protection we have as followers of Jesus in the United States, and even if our government were to become a completely totalitarian regime, we could still live an abundant life as long as we didn't look to political leaders, platforms, or policies for our ultimate security and satisfaction. We can still have hope, peace, joy, and confidence regardless of what happens in our government, as long as, like Fatima and Yaseen, we look to Jesus alone for these things, and all of our hope hinges on him.

Before we vote, then, we need to honestly ask, "Who has my heart?" The answer to this question affects not only the way we use our vote but also the way we view our lives.

The Marvelous Response

The most prominent teaching from Jesus about government comes in the midst of an exchange he had with religious leaders who were trying to trap him. Those leaders approached him with a question: "Teacher, we know that you are true and do not care about anyone's opinion. For you are not swayed by appearances, but truly teach the way of God." It was nothing short of flattery, lavishing insincere praise on Jesus for selfish reasons. Still, Jesus waited for their question.

> **"** Teacher, we know that you are true and do not care about anyone's opinion. For you are not swayed by appearances, but truly teach the way of God. **"**

"Is it lawful to pay taxes to Caesar, or not? Should we pay them, or should we not?" The religious leaders knew that if Jesus said *not* to pay taxes to Caesar, it would be an act of rebellion against the government. On the other hand, if Jesus said taxes *should* be paid to Caesar, he might appear to be compromising his devotion to God.

Seeing through their hypocrisy, Jesus said, "Why put me to the test? Bring me a denarius and let me look at it."

They brought him this coin, which was worth about a day's wage. Jesus held it in his hand, looked them in the eye, and asked, "Whose likeness and inscription is this?"

They answered, "Caesar's."

Jesus replied, "Render to Caesar the things that are Caesar's, and to God the things that are God's."

In response, the people who heard Jesus's words "marveled" at what he said (Mark 12:13–17).

Worthy of Our Hearts

Why were Jesus's words marvel-worthy? Because in addition to wisely avoiding the trap set before him, Jesus provided a revolutionary picture of how people should relate to government. Since Caesar's image was on a coin, then in a sense, that coin belonged to Caesar. Jesus affirmed what we've already seen in Scripture: God ordains government as an institution under his authority for the good of people. Therefore, we should "render to Caesar the things that are Caesar's," including taxes.

But what does it mean to render to God the things that are God's? Think of it this way. Caesar's image may have been stamped on a coin, but where is God's image stamped? The answer to that question is breathtaking, and we've seen it already in Genesis 1. God's image is stamped on every human heart. In other words, though Caesar may be worthy of a coin, God is worthy of our hearts.

| No Other Leader

No worldly leader is worthy of our hearts. No governmental authority or political party is worthy of our trust, allegiance, or hope. Nevertheless, as sinful people, we are prone to put our trust in leaders, to give our allegiance to them, and to ground our hope in them. This is our story today, and it's been the human story since the start.

For example, when God's people entered the land that he had promised to them, they immediately turned from him. In 1 Samuel 8, the nation of Israel had taken stock of the surrounding nations, and they wanted a leader to follow just like those other nations had. The elders of Israel approached the prophet Samuel and said, "Appoint for us a king to judge us like all the nations."

In response to the people, God said to Samuel, "Obey the voice of the people in all that they say to you, for they have not rejected you, but they have rejected me from being king over them." Notably, God told Samuel to "solemnly warn them and show them the ways of the king who shall reign over them." Samuel obeyed, and he warned the people, "You will cry out because of your king, whom you have chosen yourself, but the Lord will not answer you in that day" (1 Samuel 8:4–18). Put another way, the people of Israel would regret putting their trust in an earthly king.

Indeed, they did. Saul became the first king of Israel, and in his pride, he disobeyed the Word of God, damaged the people of God, and defamed the glory of God. Despite his repeated attempts to kill his appointed replacement, David, Saul was eventually deposed.

David, a man after God's own heart, became Israel's best and brightest king. Still, we know his story. He betrayed his people and lied. He stole another man's wife and had her husband murdered. If that wasn't enough, one particularly prideful decision to take a census of the people of Israel incurred God's wrath and led to the deaths of 70,000 men.

The lesson the Israelites learned from their first two kings was clear: evil leaders will let you down, and good leaders will let you down. In the words of Psalm 146:3, "Put not your trust in princes, in a son of man, in whom there is no salvation."

Only One Leader

There is only one leader who is worthy of our hearts, including our trust, allegiance, and hope. He is the Son of Man in whom there is salvation, and his name is Jesus. In a world with a history of competing leaders, Jesus's claims to kingship far outstrip any others, and his kingdom is radically different than all earthly kingdoms.

Jesus was tried for instigating rebellion, and what was his crime? His accusers said, "We found this man misleading our nation and forbidding us to give tribute to Caesar, and saying that he himself is Christ, a king." In reply, Pilate asked Jesus, "Are you the King of the Jews?" Jesus answered, "You have said so" (Luke 23:1–4).

This is the startling claim of Jesus: he is King. Yet so many of us resist this in our hearts, just like people did in Jesus's day. At the end of John's Gospel, when Pilate sought to release Jesus, the Jews cried out, "If you release this man, you are not Caesar's friend. Everyone who makes himself a king opposes Caesar." They pleaded with Pilate to crucify Jesus. When Pilate asked whether he should crucify their king, the chief priests answered, "We have no king but Caesar" (John 19:12–16).

The people repudiated Jesus as King. In fact, they went out of their way to pledge allegiance to a foreign emperor, one who had subjugated their countrymen. And in the end, Jesus was crucified because people rejected his kingship.

This makes Peter's proclamation at Pentecost all the more powerful. Filled with the Holy Spirit, Peter addressed the crowd, many of whom pledged allegiance to Caesar and called for the crucifixion of Jesus. Standing before thousands, he said, "Let all the house of Israel therefore know for certain that God has made him both Lord and Christ, this Jesus whom you crucified" (Acts 2:36). This is the fundamental confession of the church—that God has made Jesus Lord and King of all.

A Different Kingdom

To be sure, Jesus and his kingdom are very different from the kingdoms of this world. While the kingdoms of this world are built on appeasing and catering to the crowds, Jesus calls his followers to count the cost of following him. The road to Jesus's kingdom is paved not by political hostility but by spiritual humility. Entrance into Jesus's kingdom comes not by asserting yourself but by denying yourself. Instead of consolidating power through physical oppression, Jesus's kingdom offers spiritual liberation. And the citizens of Jesus's kingdom are not those who show their power with the weapons of this world, but those who place their trust in the Word of God. Jesus makes it clear: "If my kingdom were of this world, my servants would have been fighting, that I might not be delivered over to the Jews. But my kingdom is not of this world" (John 18:36).

Ultimately, the inauguration of Jesus's kingdom was not set in motion when he was elected, but when he was executed. Jesus was installed with a crown of thorns upon his head as he suffered for sin he never committed. And to this day, all (and only) those who turn from their sin and themselves and trust in Jesus as King are reconciled to God as heirs in his kingdom.

So what does all of this me
vote for political candidates and

| All of Our Trust

First and foremost, we do not
candidate or party. The unav
and party possesses weaknesses and is prone to ...
and idolatrous trajectories. No candidate or party has a monopoly
on justice. Only Jesus's kingdom—an eternal kingdom that "is not
of this world"—is ultimately worthy of our trust.

If you're reading this book, I assume you already realize that
no political candidate or party is perfect. That said, if we are not
careful, we can subtly begin to promote and defend whatever a candidate or party does. In a similar way, we can easily find ourselves
blindly supporting or habitually siding with certain candidates or
parties without biblically assessing what they are saying or standing for. What's more, we can be hesitant to hold a candidate or
party accountable when what they are saying or doing does not
align with Scripture.

We must reject this kind of political absolutism (even if unin-
tentional) because our trust resides in Jesus alone. He alone has no
weaknesses. He alone is pure and holy. He alone has a monopoly
on justice. No political candidate or party can remedy human de-

ITICAL CANDIDATE OR PARTY

CAN PROVIDE FOR US,

OTECT US, SAVE US,

OR SATISFY US.

pravity or change the human heart, and no political candidate or party can provide for us, protect us, save us, or satisfy us. Jesus alone can do these things. That's why our sole aim is his approval, not the acceptance of a political candidate or party.

All of Our Allegiance

Having Jesus as our King also means that our ultimate allegiance belongs to him and his kingdom. While we may vote or even advocate for a political candidate or party, particularly during an election season in our nation, we steward our voice and spend our lives proclaiming the gospel of Jesus's kingdom among all the nations. Our allegiance definitively belongs to God and his gospel, not our government.

Like Shadrach, Meshach, and Abednego before King Nebuchadnezzar, we would rather die than bow before any idol in this world.

Like Daniel before King Darius, we pray to God like our lives depend on it, because they do.

Like the disciples before the ruling council, when faced with a choice between standing up with a biblical gospel or shrinking back due to political pressures, we gladly say, "We must obey God rather than men" (Acts 5:29).

All of Our Hope

As the one who receives all of our allegiance, King Jesus alone is worthy of our hope. We know that he alone is sovereign, and he holds our elected leaders in the palm of his hand. We also know that every president will one day bow at Jesus's feet and confess him as Lord.

Therefore, we are not worried or panicked about elections, no matter how important they may seem. For that matter, we don't worry or panic about anything. Instead, we seek the kingdom of Jesus and his sinless righteousness with true peace and total confidence in his supreme reign. After all, we know that throughout history, leaders have risen and fallen. Presidents have come and gone. Through it all, one King alone has remained constant, and he is not up for election. Regardless of what president is chosen in our country, Jesus will be in control of it all.

The Most Important Question

So, does Jesus have your heart? This question is the most important of them all. Your answer to it will affect not just your perspective on this election but your position in eternity. Stop long enough
to consider it, to really answer it.

Does Jesus have your heart?

If the answer to that question is *no*, then I invite you to yield
your heart to him today.

DOES JESUS HAVE YOUR HEART?

IF THE ANSWER TO THAT QUESTION IS NO,

THEN I INVITE YOU TO

YIELD YOUR HEART TO HIM.

If the answer to that question is *yes*, then I invite you to realize
the weight and wonder of what it means to be a part of his body and
bride. It means that as the church, we are not for Trump, we are
not for Biden, and we are not for anyone else. It means that in any
election, the church is not for any political party or candidate. No,
we are for Jesus. All our trust is in his Word. All our allegiance is
to his mission. All our hope is in his rule today and in his promise
to return one day for those whose hearts belong to him.

QUESTION

3

WHAT DOES MY
NEIGHBOR NEED?

NOT LONG AGO, a couple of church members and I were delivering food to a family close to where I live. We drove into what seemed like a relatively nice neighborhood and arrived at what appeared to be a modest but nice four-bedroom, one-family home. The inside, however, told a different story.

We knocked on the door, and after a prolonged wait, a woman finally opened it. She was holding a child in her arms who looked to be about a year old. Recognizing us from the church, she welcomed us in with a smile. We took the groceries into the kitchen, then she invited us to have a seat on the meager furniture in the living room. There she shared her story.

Her name was Patricia. In broken English, she told us how she'd recently moved from El Salvador. Actually, *fled* would be a more appropriate term. Her husband, she shared, had been killed by Salvadoran drug traffickers. Convinced it was no longer safe for her to stay in her country, her parents sacrificed all the money they had to help her get to the United States. She came into the country with her two sons, one of whom she was holding in her lap. The other, she said, was upstairs in his room due to a severe physical handicap that makes it hard for him to even walk, much less come downstairs.

Up to that point in the conversation, I assumed Patricia and her boys were the only ones living in this house. But then she shared that she and her boys were renting a room in the house. Three other families rented the other three rooms. None of them could afford a house or even an apartment because all of them struggle to make ends meet through day labor. Instead, they shared living quarters with strangers, hoping their housemates were safe for them and their kids to be around. What's more, she shared about how she hoped her landlord was decent. She'd heard stories of women who were required to exchange "services" with the property owner when they couldn't make rent.

As I listened to Patricia share, I was struck by how close we live to one another, yet how far apart our lives are. The difficulties and potential dangers Patricia and her children face every day are drastically different than those my wife, children, and I experience. And I couldn't help but think about what I could do individually—or what we could do together—to protect Patricia and others like her from predatory landlords, to ensure equitable care for children with disabilities (like her son upstairs), and to provide a hopeful future for the baby boy in her arms.

I'll never forget that day, and I share Patricia's story in this book about voting because if we are not careful, people like Patricia will be far from our minds when we cast our ballots. Instead, we'll only have our own interests on our minds.

Consider how political campaigns are designed to appeal relentlessly to our personal preferences. Candidates and parties woo crowds with promises of a better life for *you* and *your children*. With an air of nationalistic pride, electioneers paint a picture of a superior and more prosperous country in which *you* can achieve all *your* individual dreams. As voters, we are inundated with messages about *our* rights, *our* opportunities, all the privileges *we* are entitled to possess, and all the comforts *we* deserve to enjoy.

But do we ever stop to wonder if these election messages are actually dangerous for our souls? After all, where in the Bible does Jesus beckon us with all the privileges we are entitled to possess and all the comforts we deserve to enjoy? Where does Jesus woo us with promises of everything we want in this world? When does Jesus ever encourage us to promote our nation as superior or prioritize our preferences as supreme?

Before we vote, we should pause and ask questions like, "Whose good should I promote with my vote?" and "What goals should I prioritize in my vote?" And we need to decide if our answers to these questions are driven by Jesus in his Word or by politicians in the world.

Die to Your Rights

As Americans, we love our rights. And according to Scripture, that's not all wrong. From the beginning of the Bible, God endows all people with the right to be treated honorably and judged equitably. God grants us the right to worship or reject him, to follow or forsake his Word. Such fundamental rights are part of the essence of who we are as men and women made in God's image.

But consider the rights we claim, or even demand, as Americans. We claim the right to do what we want to do, go where we want to go, live how we want to live, and achieve what we want to achieve. We claim the right to love who we want to love and marry who we want to marry. We claim the right to eat, drink, watch, wear, study, listen to, or say whatever we want. We claim the right to organize our schedule, use our time, choose our career, make our money, spend our money, take our vacation, and plan our retirement. We claim rights to safety and security, health and happiness.

In a country saturated by claims to rights, Christianity is a completely counter-cultural way of life. Just listen to Jesus's invitation: "If anyone would come after me, let him deny himself and take up his cross daily and follow me" (Luke 9:23). In a world full of rights, Jesus says, "If you're going to follow me, you must die every single day to the rights you claim in order to do anything and everything I call you to do." In other words, Jesus claims the right to determine the direction of your life and the decisions you make.

| True Life

To many, Jesus's call to lay down your rights sounds unappealing. That's the way most people heard Jesus's invitation in the first century, too. In fact, this call dispersed the crowds time and time again. But a small group of disciples stayed by his side because they believed something different. They believed that all-satisfying, all-gratifying, true, and abundant life was found not in living according to their wants but in living according to Jesus's way.

Jesus totally transformed the way the disciples thought about their lives, and he can transform the way we think about ours, too. According to Jesus, the aim of life is summarized in two statements that we began to consider in Question 1 of this book. First, life is found in loving God with all our heart, soul, mind, and strength. What an astounding aim—to experience intimacy with the God of the universe. You and I have been made to know God and enjoy him, to walk with God and worship him. The God who created us knows what is best for us, and when we trust his Word and follow his ways without condition or reservation, we will experience the life that he has designed us to enjoy.

Second, Jesus says life is found in loving your neighbor as yourself. Contrary to the pattern of this world that prioritizes *our rights,* Jesus calls us to prioritize *others' needs.* If you want to experience life to the full, Jesus says, lay down your life in love for other people. And as you do, they will experience God's love through you, and you will grow in your love for God.

Love Your Neighbor

In order to illustrate these aims in life, Jesus shared a story with a Jewish lawyer about a man traveling from Jerusalem to Jericho on a perilous road. In the story, the man was attacked by robbers. They stripped the man of all he had, beat him to a pulp, and left him for dead.

Not long thereafter, a priest came by. He knew God's law, how it required him to meet the need of a stranger. But in this story, the priest saw the man and passed by on the other side of the road.

Thankfully, another man wandered along: a Levite, or a priest's assistant. However, just like the priest, the Levite totally ignored the man in need.

After Jesus shared about the priest and the Levite, he inserted a shocking twist. "But a Samaritan," Jesus said, setting the stage. A Samaritan was a hated outsider, a half-breed whom the Jewish people believed polluted the line of God's people. When Jewish leaders wanted to discredit and offend Jesus, they called him a Samaritan. As soon as Jesus mentioned the word "Samaritan," you can imagine the lawyer's blood boiling.

The Samaritan stopped, Jesus said, and he assessed the man's need. He washed the man's wounds and took him to the nearest inn where he footed the bill for his complete care. The Samaritan prioritized and provided for everything the man needed. He stewarded his resources for the good of his neighbor.

As Yourself

Have you ever seen someone in need and stopped everything you were doing in order to care for them like this? Have you ever gone out of your way to provide everything that person needed, without question or hesitation, regardless of the cost?

I'm guessing you have. I'm guessing every single one of us has done this for somebody. And that somebody is ourselves.

We do whatever it takes to ensure that we have what we need. Or perhaps what we want. In this story, Jesus is telling us that we should love other people like that. And not just other people in general. We should love strangers like that. We should love our enemies like that. We should love them as we love ourselves.

Loving the Poor and Oppressed

Throughout the Bible, God calls his people to love others like this. In a sense, this kind of love is at the core of what it means to do justice as God requires. As we've already discussed, biblical justice is doing what's right for all people as exemplified in God's character and expressed in God's Word. But God doesn't simply leave it at "all people." Instead, he gets specific.

Biblically speaking, doing justice means not merely knowing our needs or defending our rights but taking the time to know the poor and to work toward meeting their needs. In the words of God in Proverbs 31:8–9, "Open your mouth for the mute, for the rights of all who are destitute. Open your mouth, judge righteously, defend the rights of the poor and needy." According to Psalm 140:12, we care for the poor as a reflection of the character of God who promises to "maintain the cause of the afflicted and … execute justice for the needy."

The same is true for the oppressed. A simple word search in the Bible yields over 100 references to the oppressed, highlighting God's clear concern for them. Here is a small sampling:

The Lord is a stronghold for the oppressed. PSALM 9:9

[The Lord inclines his ear] to do justice for the fatherless and the oppressed. PSALM 10:18

The Lord works righteousness and justice for all who are oppressed. PSALM 103:6

For this reason, God says to His people,

Learn to do good, seek justice, correct oppression. ISAIAH 1:17

Is not this the fast that I choose: to loose the bonds of wickedness, to undo the straps of the yoke, to let the oppressed go free, and to break every yoke? ISAIAH 58:6

Put away violence and oppression, and execute justice and righteousness. EZEKIEL 45:9

As followers of Jesus, we should oppose oppression and we should care for the oppressed in accord with the character of God and the Word of God.

Unjust Structures and Systems

Why are people poor or oppressed? As we see in God's Word, it is often due to unjust structures and systems in this sinful world. The Egyptians organized their laws and economy to enslave and oppress the Israelites. Once freed from slavery, the Israelites corrupted their judicial system and created an arbitrary legal code to exploit and mistreat the poor. The Babylonians overpowered the Israelites and subjected them to oppression in exile. Even the early church was guilty of neglecting the physical needs of Greek-speaking widows.

Amidst a world of poverty and oppression, God does not call us to let unjust structures and systems run their course. As we saw in Question 1, God calls his people in Jeremiah 22:3 and Micah 6:8 to "do justice." We are to do justice in our individual lives, as the church, and in the structures and systems that affect our neighbors in the world.

As we mentioned earlier, this is all the more applicable for followers of Jesus in a representative democracy who have a say in the laws, regulations, structures, and systems that govern our country. In his grace, God has given us a voice and a vote to promote just leaders, just processes, just laws, and the impartial execution of those laws. Applying Psalm 72 to our representative role in government, we have an opportunity to steward our voice and our vote to "defend the cause of the poor of the people, give deliverance to the children of the needy, and crush the oppressor" (Psalm 72:4).

According to God, then, my concern in voting should not just be for me and my children but also for others and their children. My children were born into a family with a dad, a mom, a stable income, access via insurance to the best medicine in the world, and access to high quality education. My children have opportunities that are substantially different from those who are born into at-risk communities with no dad or mom, no stable income, a lack of access to meaningful healthcare, and very little access to quality education. So, doing justice means working with concern and compassion not only for my family but also for others' families, and particularly poorer families. Doing justice means addressing laws, regulations, structures, and systems to better help those in need.

> **Doing justice means addressing laws, regulations, structures, and systems to better help those in need.**

Caring for Orphans and Widows

The same is true for other vulnerable groups of people, such as orphans and widows who have no family. As you read through the Bible, you see God's desire to demonstrate his power and love to these two particular groups of people. Consider these passages:

> *For the Lord your God is God of gods and Lord of lords, the great, the mighty, and the awesome God, who is not partial and takes no bribe. He executes justice for the fatherless and the widow.* DEUTERONOMY 10:17–18

> *Father of the fatherless and protector of widows is God in his holy habitation.* PSALM 68:5

> *You shall not mistreat any widow or fatherless child.* EXODUS 22:22

> *Learn to do good; seek justice, correct oppression; bring justice to the fatherless, plead the widow's cause.* ISAIAH 1:17

Voting should not just be for me and my children, but also for others and their children.

It's no surprise, then, to come to the following breathtaking verse in the New Testament, a verse that sums up God's heart for orphans and widows: "Religion that is pure and undefiled before God, the Father, is this: to visit orphans and widows in their affliction, and to keep oneself unstained from the world" (James 1:27). It's an astonishing statement. True religion apparently doesn't consist of monotonous participation in superficial pious activity. It doesn't consist in simply saying or doing the right things. True religion consists of just and consistent demonstrations of supernatural, selfless love for the poor and marginalized, particularly widows and orphans.

> **"**Religion that is pure and undefiled before God, the Father, is this: to visit orphans and widows in their affliction, and to keep oneself unstained from the world.**"** JAMES 1:27

To be clear, when the Bible describes "visiting" orphans and widows here, it means more than simply saying hello to them occasionally. This same word for "visit" in James 1:27 is used to describe how God himself visits his people to help them, restore them, strengthen them, and encourage them. To visit orphans and widows, then, means to seek them out with a deep concern for their well-being and a clear commitment to care for their needs. It means using everything at our disposal to care for them. Might that also include our vote?

Love for the Sojourner

The Bible notes another particularly vulnerable group, the "sojourners." Again, the biblical mandate to do justice applies to this discrete group.

The pages of the Old Testament present the Lord as the one who "watches over the sojourners" (Psalm 146:9). After centuries of slavery in Egypt, God told his people, "You shall not wrong a sojourner or oppress him, for you were sojourners in the land of Egypt" (Exodus 22:21). In language that follows on the heels of God's care for the orphan and the widow, God declares that he "loves the sojourner, giving him food and clothing," and consequently he calls his people to love the sojourner in kind (Deuteronomy 10:18). What's more, throughout the prophets, God accuses his people of extortion and robbery. Why? Because they have "oppressed the poor and needy," God says, "and have extorted from the sojourner without justice" (Ezekiel 22:29; see also Jeremiah 7:6; Zechariah 7:10).

The Hebrew word for "sojourner" in these passages can be translated as "immigrant." These foreigners were separated from their families and land, and they found themselves in a precarious position, in need of help from the people among whom they lived. As a result, God views them with particular compassion, and the Bible often groups the sojourner, or immigrant, alongside the orphan and the widow.

As we think about voting, there is obviously much room for discussion and debate among followers of Jesus about immigration policies and paths to citizenship in our country. Similar discussion and debate could (and should) be had about how to care well for orphans, widows, the poor, and the oppressed. But at the base of those discussions and potential disagreements is a biblical command to care for all people made in the image of God, and particularly for people in need. These are issues that, biblically speaking, are of utmost importance.

All Nations

We could continue outlining many more specific ways God calls us to do justice, but I will mention one other clear biblical emphasis on loving our neighbor because it's an emphasis that we might be prone to ignore in a national election. As we have seen in Jeremiah 29:7, God calls his people to seek the welfare of the city and nation in which they live. Further, Jesus's instruction to pay taxes to Caesar communicates appropriate support for the nation in which we live and in which our citizenship lies. Therefore, it seems biblically right and just to desire the good of our nation. Yet at the same time, if we are not careful, it is possible for nationalistic pride to keep us from compassion for all nations. There's an entire book in the Bible that reveals this reality—the book of Jonah.

Jonah was a national hero used by God to help the people of Israel strengthen their defenses against their powerful enemy, the Assyrians (2 Kings 14:25). But after his heroic work, God called Jonah to preach repentance in Nineveh, which just so happened to be the capital of Assyria. In his nationalistic pride (and hatred of the Assyrians), Jonah directly disobeyed God's call to preach in Nineveh, which led to a few nights in the belly of a fish. Once that fish spit Jonah onto the shore, Jonah went to the city, proclaimed God's Word, and the Ninevites turned to God by his grace.

> We can be more concerned about our personal desires in our own country than we are about the eternal destinies of people in other countries.

And Jonah rejoiced. Right?

Wrong.

In response, Jonah grew angry and distraught. He hated the people of Nineveh, perhaps even more now than before. In the process, Jonah became a glaring example on the pages of Scripture of how nationalistic people can work against God's global purpose.

One of the main points of the book of Jonah (if not *the* main point) is that God loves all people in all nations, even enemy nations, and God calls his people to make his grace and glory known among them all. But if we are not careful, we—like Jonah—can prioritize the good of our nation above proclaiming the gospel in other nations. We can be more concerned about our personal desires in our own country than we are about the eternal destinies of people in other countries.

A clear takeaway from the book of Jonah is that we are to work for the spread of God's love in all nations more than we are to seek safety, security, prosperity, and comfort in our own nation.

Laying Down Rights

This brings us back full circle to where we started with this question—with the issue of our rights. By God's grace, we have been given so much as citizens of the United States of America. For all that God has granted us, we should be deeply grateful. At the same time, we follow a King who commands us to lay down our rights and use the grace he has given to love our neighbors as ourselves. This, after all, is the essence of the gospel that has saved us. In the words of 2 Corinthians 8:9, "You know the grace of our Lord Jesus Christ, that though he was rich, yet for your sake he became poor, so that you by his poverty might become rich." Or, as Jesus's beloved disciple wrote, "By this we know love, that he laid down his life for us, and we ought to lay down our lives for the brothers" (1 John 3:16).

We have been redeemed from our sins and reconciled to God for all of eternity because Jesus laid down his rights for our salvation. Consequently, with his love in our hearts, it just makes sense for us to lay down our rights for the good of others.

Don't Sell Your Soul

If this is how we are to live, then is there any doubt that we should vote with these same principles in mind? Shouldn't we consider candidates and parties not based primarily upon our personal preferences, comforts, rights, or entitlements, but based on others who are in need? When we cast our ballot, shouldn't we consider both our children and others' children? Shouldn't we look for ways to lay aside our preferences for the sake of others in need, both in our nation and beyond our nation?

The poor, the oppressed, the widow, the orphan, the immigrant—they're all made in God's image. They all need God's grace. So don't sell your soul to a political party whose campaign slogans center on you. Instead, vote in a way that demonstrates supreme love for God and selfless love for others. In a world full of Patricias, dare to ask, "Who is my neighbor, and what do they need?"

QUESTION

(4)

WHAT IS THE
CHRISTIAN POSITION?

"IN MY CHURCH, voting for a Democrat could be cause for removal from the church."

I looked across the table at the pastor, wondering if my ears were playing tricks on me. Invoking excommunication over a vote? Where is that in Scripture?

This was a small gathering of good friends, most of whom were prominent pastors at thriving churches across America. Just before I dismissed the comment as an exercise in hyperbole, another leader at the table agreed. "How can a Christian," he asked, "vote for a candidate from a party that holds abortion as a key tenet of their platform?"

I considered the implications of the question. Yes, abortion is abhorrent. That's clear in the Bible (which we'll see in a moment). But is that the only issue at stake in an election? What about the scores of Christians, including overwhelming percentages of African-American Christians, who consistently vote for Democrats because of the party's record on other issues that they also deem biblically important? Can you really conclude that they lack faith in Jesus and are on a road that leads to everlasting suffering because of how they weigh those other issues? Will you really exclude them from the church because they voted for a Democrat?

It cuts both ways, of course. I've heard other people give a different version of what I heard from the two pastors around that table. "I don't see how it's possible to be a *Christian* and vote for this or that Republican candidate." I recently heard a *Christian* leader say in view of the upcoming election, "You can't be a genuine *Christian* who loves Jesus if you vote for Donald Trump." Such language—from either side—makes me wonder if we're using the word *Christian* in a way that unbiblically divides the church and ultimateley defames the name of Christ.

This leads to an all-important question regarding whether there is a Christian position on political candidates, parties, or policies. Are there any positions upon which every Christian should agree? Are there other positions upon which some Christians might disagree? And are there positions that ultimately justify exclusion from the church?

What Is a Christian?

Let's start with a definition. What is a Christian?

The question may seem too obvious or basic, but all kinds of people around the world, from cults to groups that promote counterfeit gospels, use the label "Christian" to describe things that go completely against the teachings of Christ. Various people in the United States use the label "Christian" in political discussions in order to identify positions that Christ never explicitly took. So, according to Christ, what is a Christian?

The simplest definition of a Christian is a Bible-believing, gospel-embracing follower of Jesus. Being a Christian is more than simply saying or believing true things about Christ. After all, even demons say and believe true things about Jesus, and they're most certainly not Christians. From the beginning of the New Testament, to be a Christian means to respond to Jesus's call, "Follow me," no matter the cost (Matthew 4:19).

A Christian isn't a person who follows a Christ of his own making, though. A Christian believes the Bible, for it's the Bible that truly reveals who Christ is and how he calls us to live. But according to research, almost half of all "Christians" in the United States don't believe that the Bible is completely true. Over half of "Christians" don't believe that the Holy Spirit or Satan are real, and tens of millions of professing believers don't believe that Jesus is the Son of God.[2] These "Christians" are not Christians at all. It is impossible to follow Jesus as God yet deny, disregard, discredit, or disbelieve the truths taught in God's Word.

To be clearer, a Christian embraces the gospel. The gospel is the good news that the one and only true God, the Loving Creator, Sovereign King, and Holy Judge of all has wonderfully, equally, and uniquely made all people in his image. Nevertheless, all people have rebelled against him in their sin, are separated from him by their sin, and deserve death because of sin. But God has done the unthinkable. He has sent his Son, Jesus, God in the flesh, to live a perfect and powerful life, to die a sacrificial and substitutionary death on the cross for sinners, and to rise from the grave in victory over sin, Satan, and death. As a result, anyone who repents and believes in Jesus—anyone who turns from their sin and trusts in Jesus as Savior and Lord—will be forgiven of all their sin and restored to a right relationship with God forever. This is the gospel.

A *Christian* is a Bible-believing, gospel-embracing follower of Jesus. Conversely, someone who does not believe the Bible and embrace the gospel as they follow Jesus is not a Christian.

"The Christian Position"

Unfortunately, the way *Christian* is used in political discussions is not quite so clear—or biblical. Indeed, the world at large doesn't generally understand what it means to be a Christian. As a result, the term gets tossed around with various modifiers (evangelical Christian, Catholic Christian, nominal Christian, black Christian, white Christian, etc.). And it's not just tossed around; it's used and leveraged to promote certain ideas about certain issues.

I'm guessing you've experienced this. You've heard some pundit on the news, a pastor on a stage, or a friend across the table say, "The Christian position on this issue is …." What comes next is often an opinion, or even a conviction, expressed either by a professing Christian or by a political analyst who is drawing conclusions about what professing Christians believe. Consider some examples:

The Christian position on healthcare is …

The Christian position on gun control is …

The Christian position on immigration is …

The Christian position on foreign policy is …

I could go on and on, but I trust you get the point.

The problem arises when what comes next in these sentences is not actually true for every Bible-believing, gospel-embracing follower of Jesus. After all, Jesus never actually spoke to many of these issues directly. Yet before we know it, we are attaching his name to positions he never promoted or denounced. The result?

We start judging who or what is authentically "Christian" in ways that Christ never authorized.

Clear and Direct

Now you may wonder at this point, "Isn't there a Christian position on some issues?" I'll offer a straightforward answer: absolutely, there is. Throughout his Word, God speaks clearly and directly on some issues. But there are other issues that are less clear and not as direct. Knowing the difference between these two is critically important in determining how we should use the word "Christian" in politics.

Without question, God gives many clear commands in his Word that directly apply to political issues in the world. For example, God commands people not to murder. Therefore, the Christian position on murder is simple: murder is a sin, and murderers must be punished. Likewise, as we've seen, God commands people to do justice by caring for the poor. So, the Christian position is obvious: take care of the poor. Because God creates all people with equal dignity in his image, the Christian position on racism (valuing one group of people over another based on arbitrary characteristics like skin color or hair texture) is clear: racism is evil, and we must work against it.

Consider these additional issues:

GENDER: God clearly made people as distinct men and women in his image. Therefore, the Christian position affirms these two genders as gifts of grace from God to be honored in every person.

MARRIAGE: God clearly defines marriage as a monogamous union between one man and one woman. Therefore, the Christian position is that doing justice involves defending and promoting marriage according to God's definition.

ABORTION: God's Word clearly indicates that he forms children in their mother's womb. Therefore, the Christian position asserts that abortion is the wrongful taking of a person's life.

These examples, and seemingly countless others, represent clear, direct lines from biblical truths to political positions. These truths don't just apply in our country; they apply to all countries across all of history. Wherever we are in the world, Christians—Bible-believing, gospel-embracing followers of Jesus—should universally and faithfully think, desire, decide, and act according to that which is clear and direct in God's Word.

| Less Clear and More Indirect

Meanwhile, there are a host of other issues in political discussions where we do not have a clear, direct line from biblical teaching. Instead, we would say the line is less clear and more indirect. On these issues, there is not *one Christian position* that Bible-believing, gospel-embracing followers of Jesus universally and faithfully adopt. Instead, there are *many Christian positions* that might be possible.

To illustrate the difference, consider taxes. In Romans 13:7, Paul gives a clear and direct command to honor God by paying taxes. However, though the biblical obligation to pay taxes is clear, the political position on how those taxes should be exacted is not as clear. Should we advocate for a progressive tax system or a flat tax? Should we advocate for lower tax rates or higher ones?

As Christians involved in a democracy, we should formulate positions on what we believe is most just when it comes to taxes. Still, we ought to be slow to use the phrase, "The Christian position on tax rates is …." Why? Because even in our best attempts to apply what the Bible teaches about justice, we're going outside the bounds of the clear and direct teachings of God's Word.

As another example, consider immigration. We have already concluded that God's Word commands us to care for the sojourner, or immigrant. However, we don't have verses in the Bible that tell us how many immigrants or refugees should (or should not) be admitted into our country on an annual basis. Likewise, we don't have passages in the Bible that outline what a path to citizenship should (or should not) look like. That doesn't mean these latter issues aren't important; on the contrary, they are extremely important. But we should be careful to differentiate between that which is clear in God's Word and the positions we adopt that are less clear.

Division in the Church

Earlier I mentioned that we can use the word "Christian" in ways that unbiblically divide the church and ultimately defame the name of Christ. We'll explore division in the church more in Question 6, but to at least tease the issue here, when someone claims to have the Christian position on an issue, he or she is asserting that every Bible-believing, gospel-embracing follower of Jesus should agree with that position.

As we have seen, there is a place for such statements. We have listed biblical examples, including abortion, marriage, murder, paying taxes, and caring for the poor and the immigrant. But as soon as someone uses language about the Christian position and does not have clear, direct language from God's Word supporting that position, he or she has gone beyond the bounds of the Bible and is unbiblically dividing the church. Claiming to know the Christian position draws a line in the sand. There are those who are in and those who are out.

But decisions of who's in and who's out are God's alone to make. So be careful not to take that stand and make that statement unless you can back it up with clear, direct words from God himself. Otherwise, be warned. You might be causing division in the church in a way that is contrary to God's Word.

Misrepresenting Christ

Cautions about claiming to know the Christian position reach a new level of seriousness when we consider how we're representing the name of Christ. Imagine that after your death, your closest friend claims to speak on your behalf and uses words you never spoke and wouldn't necessarily say. This would be serious cause for concern because your friend would be claiming to represent you while, in fact, misrepresenting you and potentially damaging others' impression of you in the process.

The Christian's supreme concern is the reputation of Jesus Christ. We live and die for his honor. So whenever we say, "The Christian position is …" we must be certain that it's a position that is clearly and directly expressed in the Bible. Otherwise, we will do what we have done all across our country in political discussions: we will misrepresent the Word of God and malign the glory of Jesus in the process.

"The Christian Candidate"

For these same reasons, we should never say, "The Christian candidate is …" and then insert the name of the candidate we prefer. Why? Because no verse in the Bible endorses any particular candidate in a contemporary election. What's more, like the rest of us, politicians are inherently flawed human beings. God the Father has only opened up the heavens in support of one person, saying, "This is my beloved Son, with whom I am well pleased" (Matthew 3:16). His name is Jesus, and he is the only leader whose character and platform are completely endorsed by God.

Now, you may be wondering, "What about a politician who is genuinely a Christian?" To the extent that a politician is a Bible-believing, gospel-embracing follower of Jesus, then by all means call them a Christian. However, as soon as you say, "This is the Christian candidate," many people will believe you're stating more than a simple fact. Many (or maybe most) will interpret your statement this way: "This candidate is the one whose positions and policies align with Christ." But the reality is, in our modern political system, that candidate will inevitably espouse positions and policies that God has not clearly and directly expressed in his Word (as we explored above).

For these reasons, I exhort us to use our words carefully and clearly when we're talking about a candidate. If we believe a certain candidate is better than another based on Christian values, then let us say exactly that. And if that candidate is actually a Christian, then let us simply say, "This candidate is a follower of Jesus working to make biblically informed decisions on public policy."

"God's Man or Woman"

A similar caution relates to labeling a candidate—or even a president—as "God's man or woman for this job" or "the person God has called or appointed to lead our country." When Christians hear these sorts of statements, they might again feel the pang of division if they do not support that candidate. Maybe even worse, when non-Christians hear these sorts of statements, they might believe you're saying that God endorses whatever that candidate says or does.

Consider two examples of presidents today: Donald Trump in the United States and Sahle-Work Zewde of Ethiopia (the first female President of Ethiopia). Did God call or appoint President Trump and President Zewde to lead their respective countries? It depends on what you mean when you ask that question. If you're asking, "Is God sovereign over the appointments of all leaders who govern in every nation?" the answer is a resounding yes. All throughout Scripture, God raises up leaders and deposes leaders. God is ultimately sovereign over any leader in any country. But if you're asking, "Does God personally endorse every leader who governs every nation?" the answer to that question is a resounding no.

Does God personally endorse Donald Trump or Sahle-Work Zewde, including everything they say and do? Some might say, "No, but God does endorse their policies," at which point we must ask, "Which ones?" All of them? Some of them? Or maybe just the ones we like, the ones that accord with our positions?

Let's be careful before saying that a candidate or a president is "God's person." After all, Pharaoh was "God's person" in the sense that God raised him up to show his power. Still, God most certainly didn't endorse him or his policies.

"A Gospel Issue"

Finally, consider a caution about labeling something "a gospel issue." It is not uncommon for Christians to say racism or immigration or poverty relief are "gospel issues." To an extent, these issues do indeed relate to the gospel. The gospel makes clear that God has made all people equally in his image, so racism is wrong. And those who have been saved by God's grace ought to care for the immigrant and the poor. However, calling these issues "gospel issues" runs the risk of overstepping the teaching of God's Word, implying that specific policies must be embraced by those who believe the gospel. Even worse, we run the risk of equating an issue like poverty relief with the essence of the gospel, turning the gospel into a message of social action instead of a message of divine salvation.

By all means, let's strive to take political positions that are informed by gospel foundations. But let's refrain from using language that unnecessarily, unhelpfully, or unbiblically ties the gospel to a political calculation.

Two Categories

How does all of this help us as we prepare to vote? In the next question, we'll consider how to weigh particular issues. We'll try to differentiate between what is or is not the Christian position. In other words, we'll approach each issue with two categories in mind: (a) *the* Christian position *according to God's Word* and (b) *a* Christian position *according to our wisdom.* The latter category will involve issues that are less clear in God's Word but on which, with the help of God's Spirit, we work to make the wisest political decisions possible. We will make such decisions humbly, realizing that other Christians may make different decisions. In the process, we'll hopefully promote the unity of the church and magnify the name of Christ.

QUESTION

(5)

HOW DO I WEIGH THE ISSUES?

LET'S IMAGINE a dream scenario.

You enter the voting booth on election day, and you're met with two options. The first candidate clearly represents positions that accord with God's Word. The candidate is pro-life, promotes justice for the economically disadvantaged and the immigrant, and counters racism head-on. The candidate is an exemplary follower of Jesus who tries to put God's clear commands into practice. Though the candidate's party platform involves a host of positions that cannot be said to be the Christian position, a good argument can be made that those policy positions represent a wise Christian approach.

The second candidate and party are markedly different. The candidate is openly antagonistic toward everything in God's Word and has no regard or respect for followers of Jesus and their beliefs. On almost every significant issue, the candidate works against clear commands in God's Word. What's more, the party platform contains hardly any positions that could conceivably be called a Christian position.

As you look at the options, the decision is easy. With peace of mind and a clear conscience, you walk into the voting booth on election day, and you cast your ballot for the first candidate. Simple, right?

Unfortunately, this isn't the way of the modern world. If things were so cut-and-dried in our country today, you probably wouldn't have picked up this book (though I submit that it would still be helpful to ask these seven questions). But since such simplicity is not a reality, what do we do? With a host of different issues before us, some of which are clear in God's Word and others that are less clear, and with two primary candidates and parties that have divergent perspectives on those issues, how do we weigh all the information in order to make a wise decision with our vote?

Two Parties

Let's start by reiterating a point from Question 2 about who holds our hearts. In the history of democracy, every political party has possessed both strengths and weaknesses. As products of human invention, political parties inevitably have idolatrous trajectories and trend toward positions that do not honor or reflect God's character. No human political party has a monopoly on justice.[3]

These foundational realities are important, particularly in a two-party system where followers of Jesus feel squeezed into a mold in which they don't necessarily fit. As we've seen, biblical principles are not exclusively practiced by one party or the other. And don't both political parties show evidence of God's common grace?

Questions about Opposing Parties

It might be helpful to pause here because some of you may be thinking, "I don't think that political party shares *any* biblical principles or shows *any* evidence of God's common grace." If that thought is rattling around in your brain, I would encourage you to ask the following questions:

- Are there any concepts consistent with biblical justice being promoted by the political party that I oppose?
- Does that political party show any concern for vulnerable individuals and groups?
- Does that political party demonstrate any desire for fair creation or implementation of laws?
- Do any of that political party's candidates show evidence of decency, morality, or order?
- How is that political party trying to promote good and prevent evil?

Considering these questions as they relate to a politician or a political party that you oppose may help you in a variety of ways. You may find yourself appreciating people that our political culture wants you to disparage. You may begin to discover that "those people" are not necessarily out to ruin the country, including you and everyone else in it. They may be doing what they believe is best, and most loving, and most right, even if they are seriously mistaken. In this realization, you might recall a few times when you've been mistaken, even when you thought you were promoting good. This understanding might prevent you from judging others in a way you don't want to be judged.

In an even greater way, asking these questions may draw you closer to God. If you're honest in answering these questions, you'll find yourself growing in your ability to appreciate God's grace in people who are very different from you, and even in people who might be very opposed to him. You might come to see in a fresh way that many of the people you oppose politically are sinners in need of a Savior, and they're doing the very best they know how. You might be prompted to pray for them and share the gospel with them or their political followers instead of warring with them over political opinions.

Questions about Your Own Party

A potentially more helpful exercise, though not always an easier one, is to ask similar questions of your own political party. Since we're usually prone to think more positively about candidates or parties that we are inclined to support, it can be helpful to ask questions similar to those above but with a different slant:

- Are there any concepts of injustice that might be motivating my political party?

- Does the political party I support show any lack of concern for any vulnerable individuals and groups?

- Does the political party I support demonstrate any lack of focus on fair creation or implementation of laws?

- Do any political candidates in the party I support show a lack of decency, morality, or order?

- How is my political party failing to promote good and prevent evil?

Asking and answering these questions can be a humbling exercise, particularly when it exposes realities we may not want to see. One of those realities is the tendency to judge sin in those we oppose politically while excusing sin in those we support politically.

As an example, before the 2012 election in the United States, one survey reported that 70% of people who identified as white evangelical Protestants said that an elected official's personal character was critical to his or her ability to govern ethically. Four short years later, before the 2016 election, that number had dropped from 70% to 30%.[4] Over the course of four short years, self-identified white evangelical Protestants completely shifted their views on personal character in an election. It's at least worth asking why that shift occurred.

Trade-Offs

Even as I write that last sentence, I can hear some people's response: "The 2016 election presented two candidates who were both lacking personal character." My aim in this book, again, is not to argue that point one way or the other. But the very argument itself leads us to a reality that we face as we vote in a two-party democratic system: we are making a choice between sinful candidates and imperfect parties. If both candidates and parties show evidences of God's grace in their efforts at just governance, and both demonstrate man's sinfulness in ways that lead to unjust governance, then every follower of Jesus who votes in the election must inevitably acknowledge and embrace some level of trade-offs.

In other words, followers of Jesus will inevitably vote for a candidate or party that they believe is better on certain issues than the other candidate or party. Their belief about which is better will presumably be grounded on biblical foundations. However, voting for that candidate or party may still come with some pretty heavy baggage. No matter which way you vote, you're going to support a candidate or party that may not align with biblical foundations in every possible area.

NO MATTER WHICH WAY YOU VOTE, YOU'RE GOING TO SUPPORT A CANDIDATE OR PARTY THAT MAY NOT ALIGN WITH BIBLICAL FOUNDATIONS IN EVERY POSSIBLE AREA.

Abstain from Evil

Oh boy, here we go. We're talking about the "lesser of two evils" approach to voting, right? It's the approach where we hold our nose and vote for a candidate or party we don't fully support (and may actually have serious concerns about) simply because that candidate or party is not as evil as the other. You might assume this is what I'm advocating. Am I?

Not exactly.

What's unhelpful about this "lesser of two evils" language is that the Bible gives us the following command: "Abstain from every form of evil" (1 Thessalonians 5:22). This is why some followers of Jesus may choose convictional inaction by deciding not to vote. But I don't believe convictional inaction is the only option for followers of Jesus who want to abstain from evil. It seems possible to steward our vote in a sin-soaked world in such a way that we can work toward justice in significant ways while soberly realizing that injustice remains in other ways.

Competing Injustices and Potential Compromises

Part of the effect of sin in the world of politics is competing injustices. Take, for example, a proposed law that includes substantial, needed relief for the poor yet at the same time loosens restrictions on abortion. Or consider another proposed law that tightens restrictions on abortion yet loosens the definition of marriage.

In circumstances like these, followers of Jesus should want to work for justice in every way, not just one way. Yet we find ourselves continually faced with potential compromises—times in which we must make hard decisions, and we could conceivably make a case for why (or why not) to support either side of that decision.

Biblical Clarity and Practical Consequences

As we make these hard decisions, it is helpful to weigh our options as wisely as possible based on God's Word and the situation around us in the world. And different followers of Jesus will weigh options in different ways. Consider two factors that Christians might use to weigh political options: *biblical clarity* and *practical consequences*.

The first and most important factor is *biblical clarity*. We want to hold fast to truths and commands that are clear in God's Word and that have direct application to political positions in the world. Earlier we mentioned several issues where the Christian position is unambiguous, issues like murder, care for the poor, marriage, and racism. As we look at political issues, we want to determine how direct the line is from God's Word to those issues. In our decision-making, we want to give greater weight to issues where the line is clear and direct, and lesser weight to issues where the line is less clear and more indirect.

The second factor to consider is *practical consequences*. This involves evaluating the potential consequences of the political decisions we make, including the effects of those decisions in our communities, our country, and the world. As we make political calculations, we measure the weight of practical good or harm that might come to people based upon our decisions.

| Weighing Abortion

In Question 7, I'll offer a decision-making grid for voting in light of a number of particular political issues. But for the time being, let's take just one of the Christian position issues from earlier—abortion—and consider how Bible-believing, gospel-embracing followers of Jesus might weigh this issue differently in an election.

According to Psalm 139 and a host of other Scripture passages, God knows, loves, forms, and fashions children in the womb of their mothers. Abortion, therefore, is an affront to God's sovereign authority as Creator, an assault on God's glorious work in creation, and an attack on God's intimate relationship with the unborn. For this reason, Christians should work to save children in the womb. This is the Christian position. And I should add that the Christian position is also to care for children out of the womb as well as their mothers in at-risk situations.

Years ago, in the United States, a politician could run for either of the two primary political parties and be pro-life or work against abortion. This, however, is no longer the case in our country. The Democratic Party promotes abortion, and it is almost impossible to be a Democratic politician while advocating for pro-life policy. The reverse is also true. It is highly unlikely that you'll find a Republican who promotes abortion.

Still, various Christians identify as Democrats or vote for candidates in the Democratic Party, causing other Christians to wonder, "How is it possible for any Christian to vote for a Democrat or identify with the Democratic Party?" The answer to that question is found in different Christians weighing different issues in different ways and coming to different conclusions. What do I mean?

A Plethora of Issues

No Christian would be a Democrat if the only issue involved in an election was abortion. If that was the case, then every Christian's choice would be clear. But abortion is not the only issue involved in an election, particularly for the President of the United States. Every Christian has a host of issues to weigh in a presidential election.

Consider a short and non-exhaustive list of political issues: judicial appointments, gun control, gender identity, government mandates, drug policy, social security, social media regulation, net neutrality, minimum wage, government spending, corporate tax, capital gains tax, property tax, pension reform, labor unions, tariffs, immigration, border wall, border security, campaign financing, foreign lobbying, healthcare, Medicaid, marijuana use, veterans affairs, elementary to college education, climate change, oil drilling, alternative energy, nuclear energy, space exploration, foreign aid, foreign elections, the UN, NATO, NSA, prison reform, police reform, drug trafficking, public transportation, and ... well, I trust you get the point.[5]

Might it possible, then, for a Christian to believe that abortion is biblically wrong but at the same time want to advance biblical justice in other areas? Might it be possible for Christians to support a Democratic candidate or the Democratic Party in order to stop other injustices, even while understanding that the candidate they support desires to continue abortion?

Christian Y and Z

"But we're talking about millions of babies who are dying!" you might say. "How can that even begin to compare with pension reform and capital gains taxes?" That's a good question, and this is where I hope that considering both factors above—*biblical clarity* and *practical consequences*—might be a helpful framework for understanding how *different* Christians might weigh these issues in *different* ways and come to *different* conclusions. Let's imagine two such Christians.

We'll start with Christian Y. She weighs *biblical clarity* on the issue of abortion extremely high, seeing it as the evil, horrifying murder of children made in God's image. She also weighs *practical consequences* on this issue extremely high, believing that if she votes for a Republican candidate or the Republican Party, there is a chance that abortions will end, particularly if conservative Supreme Court appointees overturn *Roe v. Wade*, the Supreme Court case that made abortion legal. That potential practical consequence, in her calculation, far outweighs almost every other injustice in our country. Even if a Democratic candidate could balance the nation's budget tomorrow and end all taxation in the process, she would still not vote for that candidate because of how she weighs abortion in terms of *biblical clarity* and *practical consequences.*

Now let's consider Christian Z. She weighs biblical clarity on abortion just as Christian Y does. But when Christian Z considers the *practical consequences* on this issue, while she desperately wants to save children in the womb, she doesn't believe voting for a Republican candidate will change the law of the land. In fact, based on history, Christian Z is suspicious of the idea that a Republican candidate will be able to put a stop to abortion. She believes that even if *Roe v. Wade* is overturned, the issue might still go back to the states, where locations that already have a high number of abortions will continue to perform them. So, she weighs the *practical consequences* of voting for either a Republican or Democratic candidate much lower than Christian Y does on the issue of abortion.

Now if abortion were the only issue in an election, then Christian Y and Christian Z would both vote to oppose abortion. Where they diverge is on the myriad of other issues at play in a presidential election. Let's add in just one other issue for now: economic policies aimed at caring for the poor.

One More Issue

Imagine that Christian Z believes that the outcome of the upcoming election is significant regarding economic policies aimed at caring for the poor. Though these issues may be a bit lower on the level of *biblical clarity* (i.e., Scripture isn't explicitly clear and direct about specific economic policies relating to care for the poor), Christian Z rates these issues particularly high in terms of *practical consequences*. Further, she believes that a Democratic candidate or party in this election will make a significant difference for the good of the poor. Based upon that conviction, in addition to her opinion that this election is not going to have significant *practical consequences* for abortion, it is reasonable that Christian Z may decide to vote for a Democratic candidate.

Conversely, Christian Y may agree that the policies of the Democratic candidate or party will likely be more effective in terms of caring for the poor. Further, Christian Y may agree on the level of *biblical clarity* associated with those policies. However, Christian Y believes that when Democratic candidates are elected, they immediately rush to loosen restrictions on abortion instead of caring for the poor. So Christian Y believes that in the end, voting for a Democratic candidate will have a low level of *practical consequences* regarding care for the poor and a high level of practical consequences for the death of children. Therefore, it is reasonable that Christian Y may decide to vote for a Republican candidate.

Based solely on these two political issues, Christian Y and Christian Z are pretty much guaranteed to vote differently in the upcoming election. Though they both embrace the gospel and are trying to apply biblical foundations to their voting decisions, they come to different conclusions. The reason? They weigh issues differently in terms of both *biblical clarity* and *practical consequences.*

Serious Consideration of the Question

I hope it's clear that I'm not asking you to agree with everything Christian Y or Christian Z represents in the above illustration. I'm also not implying that Democratic economic policies are better for the poor than Republican economic policies. Many Christians will disagree on that and many other issues. I'm simply illustrating that the question "How do I weigh the issues?" is extremely significant and requires serious, informed, biblical, prayerful consideration in our voting decisions.

We'll come back to this in Question 7 when we apply *biblical clarity* and *practical consequences* to a decision-making grid in order to answer the final question, "So how do I vote?" But before we get there, and considering the notable differences between Christian Y and Christian Z above, there's one more critical question to ask as we remember that our goal is not checking a certain box on a ballot. Our goal is faithfulness to Christ as a unified church, even as we cast different ballots.

QUESTION

(6)

AM I EAGER TO MAINTAIN UNITY IN THE CHURCH?

BACK TO THAT PRAYER on stage with the president.

In the hours and days that followed my decision that Sunday afternoon, there was no shortage of conflicting opinions expressed by professing Christians. One might conclude that I had created problems and caused division both inside and outside our church. But I wonder if another conclusion might also be plausible. Could it be that instead of creating problems, my decision uncovered problems that were already present beneath the surface? Is it possible that instead of *causing* division, my decision *revealed* division that is prevalent within the church?

The long-held view of politics and religion in the United States is that a person's faith drives their politics. In other words, the commonly accepted perspective is that a person's church involvement will determine his or her political views. However, significant research has shown that this conventional view is not true, at least not today. In the United States, particularly among rising generations, people are choosing their political position first and then determining their involvement (or, increasingly, their lack of involvement) in church. Basically, people self-select into churches (or not into churches) based upon their politics.[6] One prominent study across a variety of churches found that very few people attend church services with other Bible-believing Christians who hold different political views than them.[7]

This is tragic, and I don't use that term lightly. Followers of Jesus are dividing into different churches not based on what they believe about the Bible and the gospel, but based on what they believe about political candidates, parties, and positions. This should not be so. Before we get to our final question about voting, then, we need to ask this critical question: "Am I eager to maintain unity in the church?"

Bending over Backward

In the week following the president's visit, I immersed myself in praying for and meditating on church unity. I read the powerful language of Ephesians 4:3, in which Paul urges Christians to be "eager to maintain the unity of the Spirit in the bond of peace." Considering this verse, I wondered, "Aren't Christians supposed to bend over backward to do everything they can in order to maintain unity in the church?" Sadly, I couldn't seem to find this eagerness among professing Christians.

As I considered what it means to be eager for unity, some of Jesus's final words came to mind. Before he went to the cross, he prayed the following for all believers: "That they may all be one, just as you, Father, are in me, and I in you, that they also may be in us" (John 17:21). That week, I wanted the same kind of unity in the church that the Son and the Father experience with the Spirit in the Trinity. I want it still today.

Don't you?

Holding Together amidst Differences

I spent many hours that week studying Romans 14–15. In this letter, Paul wrote to a pretty cosmopolitan church in which followers of Jesus disagreed about food and feasting. There were people who said, "It's okay to eat meat," while others said, "We should not eat meat." There were disagreements about particular days that some thought should be honored and celebrated. Division abounded.

It seemed like these chapters were a good place to answer the question, "How can a church hold together when some members are so different from others?" There were obvious differences among the Christians at Rome. Some (those Paul labeled "strong") felt free to eat meat. Others (those Paul called "weak") didn't feel free to eat meat. The division caused all kinds of problems because each group was prone to think that the other should share their beliefs. This

> **"** May God grant you to live in such harmony with one another, in accord with Christ Jesus, that together you may with one voice glorify the God and Father of our Lord Jesus Christ. **"**
>
> ROMANS 15:5–6

division affected the ways they related to each other when, for example, they shared a meal together, or when a particular day popped up on the calendar.

How could the Roman church hold together? Paul didn't tell them to create different churches, one for carnivores and one for vegetarians. That probably would have been easier in some ways, just as it might be easier for our church in metro Washington D.C. to separate congregants by political perspective (or a variety of other distinctives). Nor did Paul recommend creating a church that was comfortable for only one group, showing preference for one group over another. Instead, Paul called the church to build unity around Jesus. He prayed that God would "grant you to live in such harmony with one another, in accord with Christ Jesus, that together you may with one voice glorify the God and Father of our *Lord Jesus Christ*" (Romans 15:5–6).

How do you do that?

What Most Honors Jesus

I think the answer the Bible gives is clear. First and foremost, when God's Word speaks clearly and essentially about an issue, believe and obey his Word. In other words, on issues where we know what the Christian position is, we should take that position. The last thing we need in the church is some vague, ambiguous, superficial, flimsy unity that has nothing to do with Jesus and his Word. No, we need a clear, specific, supernatural, rock-solid unity that is centered around Jesus and his Word.

However, as we've already seen, there are other issues that are less clear in God's Word and are not a matter of belief or obedience for every Christian. We've discussed these issues in terms of *a* Christian position. To use the language from Romans 14–15, it's possible to eat meat as a Christian, and it's possible to not eat meat as a Christian. Followers of Jesus may approach scores of issues in different ways according to their conscience.

That leads to the exhortation the Bible gives to Christians who think differently about things that are not as clear or essential in God's Word. When that's the case, the Bible calls us to do that which we believe best honors Jesus. Consider the language of Romans 14:6–8:

The one who observes the day, observes it in honor of the Lord. The one who eats, eats in honor of the Lord, since he gives thanks to God, while the one who abstains, abstains in honor of the Lord and gives thanks to God. For none of us lives to himself, and none of us dies to himself. For if we live, we live to the Lord, and if we die, we die to the Lord. So then, whether we live or whether we die, we are the Lord's.

The point is clear: in matters where Christians are free to differ, we are free to do whatever we believe most honors Jesus.

Do you know what's really interesting here? The Bible says that it's good to have strong convictions about what we believe best honors Jesus, even in situations where we disagree with other Christians. This sounds counter-intuitive to the way we might think. If the aim in the church at Rome was unity, then we might expect the Bible to say, "Don't have strong convictions on issues of disagreement." But the Bible says the exact opposite. In the words of Romans 14:5, "One person esteems one day as better than another, while another esteems all days alike. Each one should be fully convinced in his own mind."

Fully convinced—a high standard.

The Bible doesn't say, "Don't have conviction about what you should or shouldn't eat, or what days you should or shouldn't esteem." Instead, it commands us to be convinced in our own minds that what we're doing honors God. If that's abstaining from certain food, so be it. If that's eating certain food, so be it.

In our differences, it's good for us to have strong convictions about what most honors Jesus. Now you (or I) might think that such convictions make the problem worse. But they don't, so long as we follow the rest of God's Word.

Love and Listen

God tells us that on issues about which we are free to disagree, we should practice love toward one another as if we're family. "With brotherly affection," Romans 12:10 says. We should "welcome" one another and refuse to "despise" or pass unbiblical "judgment" on each other because we're "walking in love" toward one other (Romans 14:1–3, 15).

What does this mean practically? It means we listen to each other. In the words of James 1:19, we must be "quick to hear, slow to speak, slow to anger." (Maybe a modern-day paraphrase would add "slow to post or tweet.") This command is particularly appropriate in a culture that entices us at every moment to express our thoughts from behind a screen instead of looking into the eyes of our brother or sister and listening in a spirit of love.

As we listen to one another, we may realize that there are followers of Jesus in the church who think differently than us, and we may grow to respect their difference of opinion on issues that are not clearly spelled out in God's Word.

The Question that Sunday

I was presented with a question on that Sunday when President Trump visited our church. To be clear, let's clarify what the question was *not*. (There was an astonishing amount of confusion about this.) The question was not whether we should pray for the president, privately or publicly. Of course we should do that. Every follower of Jesus and every church should do that. Why? Because that's clear in the Bible. That's why I read 1 Timothy 2 before the prayer.

What was the question, then? I might phrase it this way: "Should we bring the president onto the stage in a church gathering to pray for him publicly (in front of a sea of cameras)?" Unfortunately, there's no Bible verse answering that question specifically. First Timothy 2 doesn't say, "When the president is on his way back from playing golf and stops in at the end of your church service, here's what to do." As a result, followers of Jesus who fully believe the Bible might answer that question in different ways.

One Side

On one hand, some might say that we definitely *should* bring the president on stage in that situation to pray for him. What a unique opportunity to obey 1 Timothy 2 together, and to do so publicly as an example that might encourage a lot of people to pray for him. This honors the president, which is a biblical thing to do (see Romans 13:7 and 1 Peter 2:17). Regardless of what anyone else thinks about the president, we should not only honor him, but we should also count it an honor to pray for and with him, not only in private but in public. We should pray like this for any president, regardless of party affiliation.

In addition, we shouldn't just do this for the sake of the president. We care about the good of our neighbors, so we should pray publicly with and for our government officials, that they might work for justice and mercy in our country. And when we pray, we shouldn't miss an opportunity to proclaim the gospel in prayer.

I don't presume that this exhausts all the reasons why one might say that praying for the president publicly was a good idea, but as best as I can tell in those fleeting seconds backstage, many of these reasons informed my decision.

Another Side

At the same time, other followers of Jesus might say—with the same level of conviction—that we should pray for the president both privately and publicly in our worship gathering. After all, it's biblical. But they would say we should not bring the president on stage in that situation.

Why not?

So much of politics is about appearances, and by calling a public official to the stage, we're taking a holy moment in a worship gathering and turning it into a public spectacle. Politicians, media, or throngs of social media users can and will twist, use, and abuse this event for all kinds of purposes. Some (maybe many) might view the act as our church's endorsement of the president or all of his policies. At the very least, they might assume this symbolizes the pastor's endorsement of the president or all of his policies. In addition, standing with the president on the stage might be extremely discouraging to at least some (maybe many) members of the church who disagree with some (maybe many) of the president's policies, words, or actions.

This is to say nothing of those outside the church who are already skeptical because they have seen so many ways in which the church has been co-opted by political parties and personalities. When they hear the news that our church hosted the president on stage, it will turn them away. They'll want nothing to do with our church, and their exposure to the gospel will be limited.

On top of that, what about the clear biblical warning in James 2 not to show favoritism or preferential treatment in the gathering of the church? Or consider the biblical precedent of challenging leaders in political positions. John the Baptist didn't hesitate to do this, and he lost his head for it. If you're going to bring the president on stage, why would you not speak more clearly about what God's Word says to him?

In the end, just ask the question, "Does bringing the president on stage lead the church toward greater unity in the gospel?" If not, then don't do it.

Unity in Our Diversity

Again, I don't presume that I've come close to exhausting the reasons why some would argue I *should* or *should not* have invited the president onto the stage for public prayer. My point is simply to say that it is possible for Bible-believing, gospel-embracing followers of Jesus to have different convictions about this decision. And it's possible that convictions on both sides of this decision might be grounded in the gospel and focused on the unity of the church. One side says to bring the president on stage for the advancement of the gospel (in one way), and the other side says not to bring the president on stage for the advancement of the gospel (in another way). One side says, "We need to be unified in *bringing* the president up," and the other side says, "We need to be unified by *not bringing* the president up."

So how do we maintain unity when we come to opposite conclusions based on biblical convictions? According to God, we stop and listen to each other in love. Sadly, this doesn't happen very often these days. The reactions and the resulting arguments surrounding my decision prove as much. In the days after that Sunday, more than a handful of people came to me saying, "Don't listen to *those people* in the church who think *this* or *that*." As I listened, I remember thinking, "*Those people* are our brothers and sisters, whom we love. At the very least, shouldn't we listen to them?"

The fact that I heard from both sides on this decision was, I believe, a good sign. It reminded me that many people in my congregation disagree with one another, but we're committed to experiencing unity together in Christ. This is not the case in many American churches. According to research we've already referenced, we divide into churches based on political convictions, and we only surround ourselves with people who think like us. Along the way, we subtly become convinced that our convictions are the *only* convictions—or at least the *right ones*. Without knowing it, we create a false unity in the church based on political convictions instead of true unity around Christ and his Word.

This might be an appropriate time to pause and ask yourself, "How many close relationships do I have with followers of Jesus whose political convictions differ from mine (assuming those political convictions have biblical foundations)?" If you don't have many (or any), then I want to encourage you to cultivate those kinds of relationships. Otherwise, we run the risk of deceiving ourselves into thinking that we have unity with other Christians around the gospel when, in reality, our unity is around a political ideology with Christ on the side.

A Different Way to Relate

As we listen to each other's diverse perspectives in the church, we learn from one another. We ask genuine questions and carefully avoid unhelpful assumptions. We intentionally resist the temptation to assemble and attack straw men.

What's a straw man? It's a form of argument that involves manipulating someone's arguments or ideas, even caricaturing them, and then attacking those words and ideas as if that's what the other person actually believes. I've had this done to me countless times, and I'm pretty sure I've done it to others. It's an easy way to castigate someone else and assert our superiority over them instead of listening and honestly responding to their actual convictions.

Amidst our disagreements and differences on those things that are less clear in God's Word, God calls us to relate to one another in a way that is very different from the world's approach. We aren't to manipulate others or make straw man arguments. Jesus beckons us to share our differences with humility, honesty, affection, sympathy, patience, kindness, gentleness, tenderness, and selflessness. He commands us to communicate with and about one another through speech that is gracious, fair, encouraging, edifying, never slanderous, and always seasoned with salt. He calls us to bear with one another in love, assume the best about one another by God's grace, and care for one another with the attitude of Christ, always looking for opportunities to please one another instead of ourselves (Romans 15:1).

For Pastors

Before we draw this question to a close, I want to offer specific encouragement to pastors. Based on all that we've explored so far, I'm compelled for the sake of Christ and his church to encourage you (pastor) to make *the Christian position* clear, not *your political conviction*. And as you do, be clear about the ways in which Bible-believing, gospel-embracing followers of Jesus might differ when it comes to their (and your) convictions.

If unity in the church revolves around Jesus and that which is clear in his Word, and if the primary responsibility of a pastor is to preach and teach God's Word, only binding the consciences of people to believe and live according to it, then we as pastors must be extremely careful with the words we use. When we preach Mark 1:15, "Repent and believe in the gospel," we are telling people to follow Jesus, for we know without a doubt that their eternity hinges on their response to him. That's what I mean by "binding the consciences of people" with that which is clear in God's Word.

In this way, pastors *should* speak authoritatively on issues that are clear in God's Word, but they *should never* speak authoritatively on issues that are not clear in God's Word. Pastors should never bind the consciences of others with their personal convictions, opinions, or preferences. In other words, we as pastors do not have the right or authority to stand before the people of God and call them to vote for a certain candidate, take a certain position, support a certain policy, or participate in a certain activity unless we can show clearly in God's Word that every Christian *should* believe or act in that way. In other words, we are responsible to God for promoting *the* Christian position, not *our* political conviction.

This is significant not just for the sake of those in our churches, but also for the sake of those outside our churches. If we are only attracting people from one political party or perspective to our church, then we are likely overemphasizing our convictions and, by default, underemphasizing that which is clear in God's Word for every Christian. Even more importantly, we represent Christ to the world as leaders in the church, and we must never dilute our proclamation of him and his Word with the promotion of candidates, groups, or platforms in this world. Pastors, for Christ's sake, let's never tie his majestic glory or matchless name to a mere politician or party.

Otherworldly Community

In a world where Christians divide into different churches over political candidates, parties, and positions, we have a unique opportunity to show that there's another way. To show that the church of Jesus Christ is a distinct and otherworldly community that transcends political party and preference. Don't you want that kind of unity? If so, don't let this election, and the choices you and other

Christians make, divide you from one another. Take the time to listen to, learn from, and love one another, particularly those who differ from you.

Love one another, knowing that one morning we will wake up with no idea that we are about to meet face-to-face with the King. We'll be going about our day, business as usual, and instead of a voice calling us from behind a stage, we'll hear a trumpet boom from the sky. In that moment—the moment we've been waiting for our whole lives—we will see the face of Jesus. This is true for all who have trusted in Jesus. Even those with whom we disagree politically.

> Take the time to listen to, learn from, and love one another, particularly those who differ from you.

We won't have any problem making a unified decision on that day. All who have followed Jesus, from every nation, tribe, and language, will fall on their faces in adoration as they enter into eternal joy under his rule and reign. So let's be eager as Christians to maintain our unity as the church today in view of that final day so that the world will know that Jesus alone is King.

QUESTION

7

SO HOW DO I VOTE?

WE'VE COME to the final question. Before we attempt to answer this question or arrive at a conclusion, let's recap.

> **1** God calls us to steward our vote for the sake of his commands, including his commands to do justice, subject ourselves to and support government, seek the welfare of our nation, and love our neighbors as ourselves.

> **2** The most important decision we can make is to yield our hearts to Jesus, placing all our trust, allegiance, and hope in him alone.

3 The driving force in how we vote is supreme love for God and selfless love for others, both in our nation and throughout the world.

4 We work to know *the* Christian position on issues that are clear according to God's Word in order to form *a* Christian position on less clear issues that require our wisdom.

5 Before voting, we weigh issues in terms of factors like biblical clarity and practical consequences.

6 No matter how we vote, we are eager to maintain the unity of the church around Jesus and his Word, not around our personal political convictions.

Based on our answers to the six previous questions, what is the answer to the seventh question, "So how do I vote?" I'll attempt to help you answer this question first with a practical tool and then with some final biblical truths.

| A Grid

In Question 5, we explored how different Christians weigh different electoral issues in different ways, leading them to different conclusions. Specifically, we explored how two particular factors—*biblical clarity* and *practical consequences*—might affect our political calculations. It's my hope that considering both of these factors will help us as we vote amidst a two-party system of American politics in which our convictions may not always completely align with either of the parties or candidates in an election.

I want to make clear that the grid I'm about to propose is not "biblical" in the sense that the Bible explicitly teaches such a grid. As we've already seen, the Bible doesn't give us detailed instructions for voting in a democratic election. This is simply my attempt to provide a practical tool as you contemplate how to vote first and foremost according to God's Word, and then according to the implications of your vote for people in the world.

By focusing on both *biblical clarity* and *practical consequences*, let's create a grid that could help in our decision-making. Consider the following:

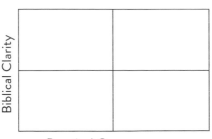

To explain how we might use this grid, envision political issues in one of the four quadrants above as you approach a particular election. If you perceive high *biblical clarity* on an issue, then you would place that issue high on this grid (i.e., in the upper half, corresponding to "Biblical Clarity" on the vertical axis). Likewise, if you perceive significant *practical consequences* relating to this same issue in a particular election, then you would place that issue far to the right on this grid (i.e., the right half, corresponding to "Practical Consequences" on the horizontal axis). In other words, you would plot that issue as follows in Figure 1:

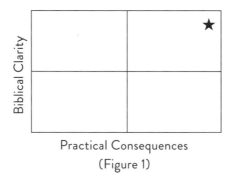

Practical Consequences
(Figure 1)

As an opposite example, if you perceive low *biblical clarity* about an issue (in other words, Scripture does not speak clearly or directly to that particular issue), then you would place that issue low on this grid (i.e., in the lower half, corresponding to "Biblical Clarity" on the vertical axis). And if you believe there are relatively insignificant *practical consequences* related to the issue, then you would place that issue far to the left on this grid (i.e., the left half, corresponding to "Practical Consequences" on the horizontal axis). In other words, you would plot that issue as follows in Figure 2:

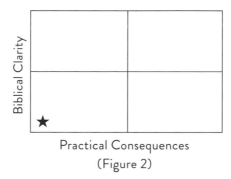

Practical Consequences
(Figure 2)

As you compare the two grids above, you would give much greater weight in your decision-making to a political issue that is in the upper right quadrant (see Figure 1). If the Bible is exceedingly clear about an issue, and you perceive the practical consequences of that issue in an upcoming election to be extremely significant, then you would likely weigh that issue very heavily in your decision-making. On the other hand, if the Bible doesn't speak clearly to a political issue, and that issue has minimal practical consequences, it would be in the bottom left quadrant (see Figure 2), and you would likely not weigh it heavily in your decision-making.

As an example, let's recall Question 5, in which we considered two Christians' opinions on the issues of abortion and economic policies aimed at care for the poor. Christian Y looked at an election and saw abortion as an issue with high *biblical clarity* and high *practical consequences*. In other words, Christian Y believed that the Bible's teaching on abortion is extremely clear, and the practical stakes of abortion in the upcoming election are extremely high. At the same time, Christian Y perceived economic policies aimed at care for the poor as moderately high in terms of *biblical clarity* but significantly low in terms of projected *practical consequences* in the upcoming election. Using "S" for "Social Issues" (including abortion) and "Ec" for "Economic Issues" (including care for the poor), Christian Y's grid when it comes to these two issues is as follows:

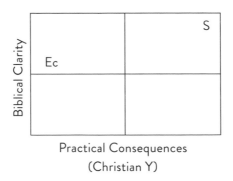

Practical Consequences
(Christian Y)

Based upon this grid, Christian Y puts a much heavier emphasis on the social issue of abortion in an upcoming election, and much less emphasis on economic policies. In other words, if she is only considering these two issues, then Christian Y will likely vote for the candidate who most closely resembles her position on abortion.

However, if you'll remember, Christian Z's perspective was different. While she completely agrees that abortion is an issue around which there is high biblical clarity, Christian Z feels that the *practical consequences* of this election on abortion are not as high, so she puts "S" for "Social Issues" (such as abortion) at a much different place on this grid. Moreover, even though she perceives that economic policies aimed at care for the poor have less *biblical clarity* around them, she believes that the *practical consequences* of these economic policies are extremely high in an upcoming election. As a result, Christian Z's grid looks very different:

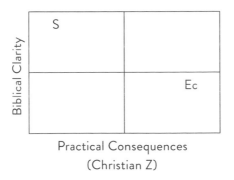

Practical Consequences
(Christian Z)

Based upon how Christian Z weighs these two issues as they appear on this grid, she may decide to vote for the candidate that she believes will bring the most positive good to the poor, even if she disagrees with that candidate on the social issue of abortion.

Eight Issues

The above discussion only takes two issues into account, and as we have said, most elections (and particularly presidential elections) involve multitudes of issues. So let's imagine Christian Y and Christian Z factoring in additional issues and then we'll consider what that might mean for their voting decision in the upcoming election.

For simplicity's sake, I'll organize political issues in the next presidential election into eight groups (listed here in alphabetical order):

- Domestic Policy Issues (including Education, Gun Control, and Criminal Justice)

- Economic Issues

- Environmental Issues

- Foreign Policy and National Security Issues

- Healthcare Issues

- Immigration Issues

- Personal Character and Morality Issues (Party Leaders, including the President and Vice President)

- Social Issues (including Sexuality, Marriage, Abortion, and Religious Liberty)

Now let's consider how Christian Y and Christian Z might weigh these issues using this grid. We will use the first letters of the words above as markers on the grid:

D = Domestic Policy
Ec = Economy
En = Environment
F = Foreign Policy and National Security
H = Healthcare
I = Immigration
P = Personal Character and Morality
S = Social

Keep in mind throughout this illustration that both Christian Y and Christian Z are Bible-believing, gospel-embracing followers of Jesus. I should also clarify that this illustration is merely hypothetical. Neither of these fictional followers represents my precise personal views, and I am not trying to persuade anyone toward either option. I am simply offering an illustration of how this grid might be used.

Christian Y and Z

Let's start with Christian Z this time. Out of all the issues in this election, she attributes the most weight to the personal character and morality of party leaders (P). She believes the next four years in this country (and far beyond the next four years) necessitate leaders whose decency and demeanor set the tone for civil dialogue about issues that matter. As stated before, she believes the time is ripe for economic (Ec), domestic (D), and healthcare (H) policies that address poverty in our country, and she believes this election will also have significant consequences for immigration reform (I). Also, as a reminder, she hates abortion, but she does not believe this election will have significant consequences for that issue. Even still, she places social issues (S) higher in terms of practical consequences (in relation to the grid above) when she considers other social issues at stake, like religious liberty and sexuality. Finally, she thinks this election has moderate implications for the environment (E) and foreign policy (F).

Admittedly, it is impossible to summarize one's perspective on political issues in one paragraph, but assuming what's stated above, Christian Z's grid might look like this:

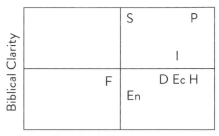

Practical Consequences
(Christian Z)

Based upon this grid, Christian Z will put the most weight on the personal character and morality (P) of party leaders. She will then weigh which candidate or party most aligns with what the Bible teaches on social issues (S), particularly issues that she perceives have the most significant practical consequences in this election. She will then consider which candidate or party she believes has the strongest view on immigration (I), followed by healthcare (H), economic (Ec), and domestic policy (D) issues. Finally, she will consider the positions of candidates and parties on the environment (En) and foreign policy (F). Using this grid, she will begin to evaluate which candidate or party is strongest on the issues that she weighs heaviest.

Christian Y, however, has a much different grid. Christian Y also believes that personal character and morality (P) are biblically clear and practically significant. However, Christian Y believes that the social issues (S) at stake in the upcoming election—from

abortion to sexuality to religious liberty—have significantly greater implications on the fabric of society than any leader's personal
character and morality. Christian Y perceives significant practical
consequences for foreign policy (F) in this election, and she sees
immigration reform (I) as a needed priority both biblically and practically. While she understands the need for better economic policy
(Ec) to care for the poor, she doesn't envision particularly significant practical consequences on that issue in this election. She sees
even less biblical clarity and practical consequences in this election
for healthcare (H) and the environment (En), and she moderately
weighs various domestic policy (D) issues.

As a result, Christian Y's grid looks something like this:

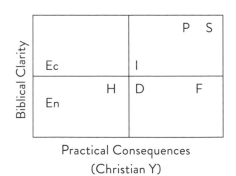

Practical Consequences
(Christian Y)

Based upon this grid, Christian Y will put the most weight on
the candidate and party that she believes represents biblical positions on social issues (S). She will then consider candidates and

parties through the lens of personal morality and character (P), though she will give less weight to that issue than to social issues. She will likely consider positions on foreign policy (F) next, then immigration (I), then domestic policy (D), then healthcare (H), then the economy (Ec), and lastly the environment (En). Using her grid, she will evaluate which candidate's or party's positions most align with hers on the issues she perceives as most significant.

Your Grid

Now fill out your own grid. Start with these same eight political issues. Feel free to add more if you like. Rate each one in terms of *biblical clarity* and *practical consequences* in the upcoming election. Your grid might change as you learn more about the candidates, parties, and issues at stake over the course of the election cycle. That's okay. This is meant to be a continuing exercise, something

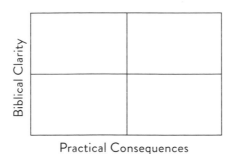

Practical Consequences

that can be updated in real time. Still, plot an initial chart to get familiar with the exercise.

Now imagine completing your grid as you approach the day when you will cast your vote. Start in the upper right corner with issues marked by high *biblical clarity* and *practical consequences*. Consider which candidate or party offers the best chance of aligning with Scripture and achieving justice on these issues. Then begin considering the other issues based on where they appear on your grid, looking first to *biblical clarity* and then to *practical consequences*. As you do, maybe your choice of candidate or party will start to become clear.[8]

Or maybe it won't. Maybe you will come face-to-face with those difficult trade-offs and compromises. Maybe you will encounter that sinking feeling as you say to yourself, "I can make a case for or against both candidates and both parties." Hopefully, however, you will have a clearer picture of the issues that you need to weigh most heavily and consider most prayerfully.

So do that. Regardless of how clear or unclear your decision seems, lay your decision before God in prayer. Seek him with all your heart. Like a child looking into the eyes of a loving Father, ask him to calm your concerns and calibrate your conscience according to his Word, his Spirit, and the wise counsel of brothers and sisters in Christ. And if your decision-making is different from those brothers and sisters, commit to loving them anyway, despite your disagreement. Commit to unity around Christ.

| Promises from God

This process of decision-making leads us to my landing point. Consider God's promises in Proverbs 3:5–8:

> *Trust in the Lord with all your heart,*
> *and do not lean on your own understanding.*
> *In all your ways acknowledge him,*
> *and he will make straight your paths.*
> *Be not wise in your own eyes;*
> *fear the Lord, and turn away from evil.*
> *It will be healing to your flesh*
> *and refreshment to your bones.*

These verses have been a perpetual encouragement to men and women of God throughout the ages because they are a powerful reminder that God will faithfully lead his people when they fear and trust in him. Even people who are mired in the division and confusion of a democratic election.

Consider God's promise in James 1:5–7, too. As we face a significant decision, one worth wrestling over, the Bible encourages us with these words:

> *If any of you lacks wisdom, let him ask God, who gives generously*
> *to all without reproach, and it will be given him. But let him ask in*

faith, with no doubting, for the one who doubts is like a wave of the sea that is driven and tossed by the wind. For that person must not suppose that he will receive anything from the Lord; he is a double-minded man, unstable in all his ways.

What an amazing promise. God will give us wisdom when we ask. If that's the case, we should ask!

While I hope this book has been helpful for you, my deeper hope is that it drives you to spend time alone with God. I hope you plead with him in prayer for wisdom regarding how to steward your vote. Nothing—absolutely nothing—can replace that time with him when no one else is around. I genuinely hope that this decision about how to use your vote draws you into deeper intimacy with God. I believe it will if you'll let it.

Radical Trust in God

Finally, I'd like to leave you with Paul's encouragement to the Romans. In the middle of that contentious environment in which Christians were adamant in their differing convictions, Paul attempted to comfort them, writing, "For whatever does not proceed from faith is sin" (Romans 14:23). It's a powerful verse that provides a penetrating definition of sin. We sin whenever we do anything that is not the fruit of trust in Jesus. There are so many implications of that last sentence (implications that would take volumes to unpack), but let's apply it to the issue of voting.

I trust we all want to glorify God with our vote. I'm guessing that at least some of us are afraid we might make the "wrong" decision. I've struggled with that before, with wondering whether I made the wrong decision. But as I think about that question, I believe Romans 14:23 teaches us that the way to sin on election day is to steward your vote apart from faith in Jesus. And that's the primary thing I want to exhort you *not* to do.

Do not be faithless on that day when you cast your ballot. Do not trust in yourself on that day. Do not trust in a candidate or a party on that day. Do not trust in anyone or anything but Jesus on that day. Make the stewardship of your vote the overflow of radical trust in Jesus, his Word to you, his Spirit in you, his rule over you, and his reign not only in our nation, but over all the nations.

When you hold your ballot in your hand, pause and thank Jesus for his loving leadership of your life and his sovereign lordship over this election. Then, as you check that box, offer this simple and sincere prayer: "Lord, may your kingdom come."

Acknowledgments

As I consider everything that happened to bring this short book together, I praise God for many people on many levels.

I praise God for the entire Radical crew, including Chris, Warren, Jackie, David, Mandy, and Bryce, who together learned how to publish a book practically overnight.

I praise God for Jason Wallis, Rob Jackman, and Kobus Johnsen for stepping in with grace and skill to make this book available to as many people as possible.

I praise God for Sealy's encouragement and example, exemplifying the heart of this book with his life.

I praise God for Seth's willingness to interrupt his family vacation (thanks, Haines family!) to take on this editorial project with practical wisdom, biblical conviction, and careful insight, all on a tight timeline.

I praise God for McLean Bible Church, a people I love and long to shepherd faithfully with God's Word amidst the challenges of this world.

I praise God for my family. Their love for me, patience with me, encouragement of me, and prayers for me make me the most blessed man in the world. This book is the fruit of sacrifices they have made, and I love and cherish them beyond words.

Ultimately, I praise God for the gospel. I shudder to think of where I would be if Jesus had not died for me. I love him as my life, and I pray this book edifies his church and glorifies him as the only King who is worthy of our allegiance.

Notes

1   For a fuller treatment of biblical foundations of governance and their practical implications (including some that I flesh out in this book), see Jonathan Leeman, *How the Nations Rage: Rethinking Faith and Politics in a Divided Age* (Thomas Nelson, 2018).

2   Barna Group, "Most American Christians Do Not Believe That Satan or the Holy Spirit Exist," April 10, 2009.

3   In this statement and the paragraphs that follow, I do not mean to imply that all political candidates and parties stand on equal moral footing. Inevitably, different candidates or parties will align more or less with biblical foundations in ways that will (and should) affect a Christian's vote.

4   Public Religion Research Institute, "Backing Trump, White Evangelicals Flip Flop on Importance of Candidate Character," October 19, 2016 (https://www.prri.org/research/prri-brookings-oct-19-poll-politics-election-clinton-double-digit-lead-trump/).

5   While the aim of this book is not to examine each of these issues, I certainly want to encourage prayerful, thoughtful, and humble consideration of these and other issues based on God's Word and the situation around us in the world.

6   Niskanen Center, "How Americans' Politics Drives Their Religious Views," November 8, 2018 (https://www.niskanencenter.org/how-americans-politics-drives-their-religious-views/). See also Michele Margolis, *From Politics to the Pews: How Partisanship and the Political Environment Shape Religious Identity* (University of Chicago Press, 2018).

7   LifeWay Research, "Many Churchgoers Want to Worship With People Who Share Their Politics," August 23, 2018 (https://lifewayresearch.com/2018/08/23/many-churchgoers-want-to-worship-with-people-who-share-their-politics/).

8   In order to keep this book relatively brief, I have not explored all the factors you might weigh in your voting decision. One such factor I have not explored in-depth is the extent to which voters are drawn to a particular candidate or party, or both. Some may like a certain candidate but dislike the platform of the candidate's party. Others may dislike a certain candidate but like the platform of the candidate's party. Different Christians may come to different conclusions about how to weigh individual candidates and political parties in their voting decisions. For this reason, I have intentionally used the language of "candidate or party" in this paragraph and throughout the book.

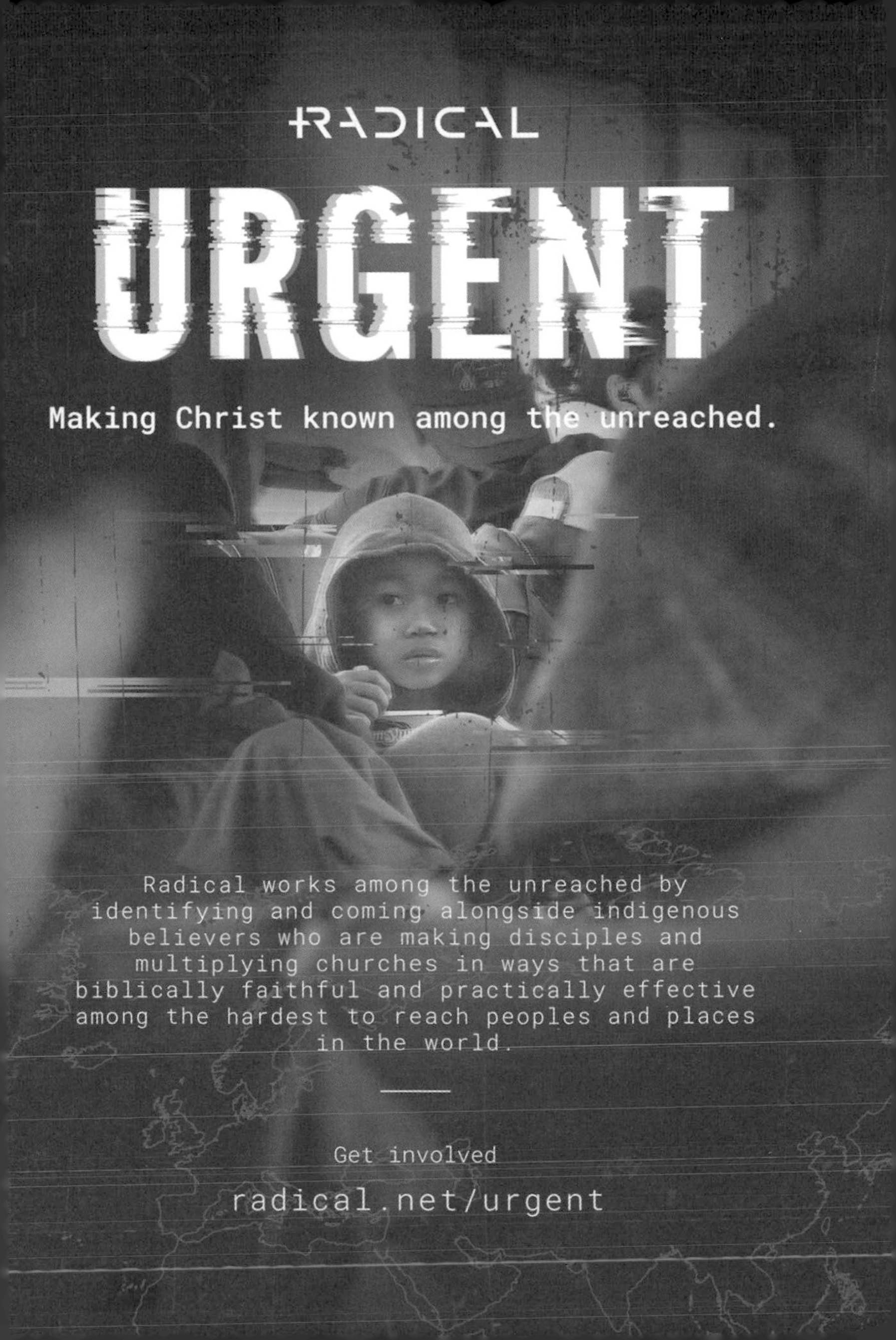
RADICAL
URGENT
Making Christ known among the unreached.
Radical works among the unreached by identifying and coming alongside indigenous believers who are making disciples and multiplying churches in ways that are biblically faithful and practically effective among the hardest to reach peoples and places in the world.
Get involved
radical.net/urgent

RADICAL

For His glory

Radical serves the church by producing biblical resources and working to equip followers of Christ to meet urgent spiritual and physical needs.

RESOURCES   EVENTS   EQUIPPING   ENGAGEMENT

Learn more:

RADICAL.NET